AMERICAN MASTER

American Master

A Portrait of Gore Vidal

James Edmonds

Those who shake the State are easily the first to be engulfed in its destruction. The fruits of dissension are not gathered by the one who began it: he stirs and troubles the waters for other men to fish in

– Montaigne
(I: 23)

Preface to the 2nd edition

RAVELLO, NOVEMBER 16, 2012. I am waiting. It is the third or fourth day since I was supposed to go out to La Rondinaia. Mr. Palumbo, the owner or at least the man with the keys to the series of gates behind Rufolo, is recovering from some long trip. The weather has been uncharacteristically sunny all week. On Friday Palumbo is finally ready and it's raining. I brace myself for whatever is down the path – I had been warned about the villa's condition – and try not to allow the wet to color my impressions.

The town is as I like it: quiet, the superfluous day-trippers snap their pictures, adjust their fanny packs and are gone. Life goes on, but the town lives on and off past glory. It was like a movie set. All the scenery was in place, but the actors had long since gone home.

This coast has seen better days. Ravello is not just the 700 people in the center but the 1,800 who spread down the mountainsides in every direction. None of them have cash. All their value is in their properties, but who wants to leave? The young don't want to return to agricultural work in the slow times. Better to work hard in the tourist season and live off the government for the rest of the year. The walk down to Amalfi tells the story: increasing numbers of terraces are left unattended. The weeds grow over and they die. It is tragic.

Those in the center are more prosperous. Anna-Maria makes her sandwiches and gossips at the emporia. Young workers do restoration work and plant spring flowers. Netta waves as she throws a bone to the cats of Via Roma. I have returned so often I think she remembers me. She works too hard, people say. The restaurant ends with her. The idiot nephew is worthless.

That Friday I meet Palumbo, a taciturn and cool man, at Hotel Eva (which he owns, along with Hotels Maria and Giordano). He is a struggling hotelier, and not even among the richest citizens. I had been warned that he was growing dotty with age. As he opens the first gate behind Rufolo he mutters how his two partners have resisted his plans for the villa. "I'm fighting them," he says defiantly.

Vidal's lonely final years in Ravello were spent on what he jokingly called "his true genius" – real estate. The villa had been his home for more than 30 years and, like a king making provisions for the succession, he was keen to ensure the kingdom did not fall into the wrong hands, in this case, his neighbors. This most aristocratic quarter of Ravello is dominated by the Villa Cimbrone, which sits perched at the top of the cliff above La Rondinaia. Cimbrone is owned by the Vuillemeir family, with whom Vidal had feuded for many years. A tall set of stone pines obscure the view of his property from Cimbrone and this is no coincidence.

When it became known that Vidal was going to sell the Cimbrone group made what the villagers considered a very fair offer. But Gore was convinced that "those peasants" were attempting to buy too much of the town. Palumbo, who had often acted as an intermediary, provided a solution. He brought in two wealthy partners and they made an offer as a group (Palumbo has a very minor stake). The figure was 10 million euros. Vidal returned to the Hollywood Hills and Palumbo began a scheme to convert the villa into a boutique hotel. Then the economic crisis hit and Palumbo's partners became reticent. Great sums were being sunk into a property without suitable parking (there was talk of building a car lift into the mountain). Vidal, bitter and facing the onset of senility, was pleased the Palumbo wasn't prospering.

As I walked with Palumbo down the private road to La Rondinaia it was abundantly clear why Vidal loved this place. This corner of Magna Graecia was once considered sacred to the god Pan. The terraces go on, the cypress allée remains enchanting, the pool is full of leaves. We pass through the last gate and enter the garden. The stone lion still stands guard. Palumbo ushers me into the house, the front foyer opening on to a long hallway. The first door on the left was his office. The desk and typewriter are still there. A bookshelf filled with rare editions, his entire oeuvre from what I could tell. I didn't dare sit.

The rest is a blur. The bedrooms and balconies. The sense of vertigo. The rain. Dusty furniture and exposed wires hanging from the walls. A tangerine from one of Vidal's trees. Palumbo offered a piece, tasted them himself, said they weren't ready. I thought the fruit tasted fine. But as we walked back to the village the taste turned bitter. The villa was no longer his. He was gone and all that remained was a shell, gutted and soulless, populated by ghosts. I was relieved when we reached the piazza.

1

ONE SPRING MORNING, a few years ago, I was driving south on the A3 from Naples. The weather was wet and had been so for days. The foreboding bulk of Vesuvius was barely visible out the window. Soon the car began to climb precipitously into the Lattari Mountains. The pressure changed and the temperature grew colder. We made one switchback turn after another, leaving the plain of Naples behind and far below. We climbed and descended through the Lattari peaks, passed through the village of Tramonti, and finally came around the bend into Ravello.

A village of about 2,500 people, Ravello clings on the side of a mountain like a sort of balcony a thousand feet above the Tyrrhenian Sea. As I checked into the hotel, the weather began to clear. Ravello and the entire Costiera Amalfitana has long drawn visitors, largely because of this illusion of perpetual summer. Nature blessed the place with a light blue sky, a sea of darker sapphire. On sunny days, horizon and sky seem to melt into one. In the distance, one can make out the outline of the Calabrian hills. The light reflecting off the water or the limestone cliffs can be damaging to the eyes.

Humankind has done the rest, terracing the mountainsides — seemingly defiant of occupation — with lemon and olive groves, clumps of cypress, palm. The vines of Virginia creeper or scrolls of Bougainvillea spill from the balconies and terraces. Even in the depth of winter, the houses and palazzos exude warmth. They are painted in earth tones — mustard yellow, salmon pink, pumpkin orange, and Pompeian red.

Ravello and the neighboring towns are dense, labyrinthine clusters — a legacy of Saracen rule, seen everywhere, especially in the narrow streets largely inaccessible to cars. One has the sense of being a guest in a large home run by a boisterous family. The same families have lived here for many centuries, including Palumbo, Mansi, and Amato.

We had arrived too late for lunch and by the evening were famished. We made our way through the tunnel and into the town piazza. To our right was the 11th-century duomo, dedicated to Ravello's patron saint, San Pantaleone. Around another corner was the entrance to Villa Rufolo, built in the 13th century for the merchant family of the same name. Down Via Roma, a little side street down from the duomo, we ate at Cumpa Cosimo, a simple trattoria that has been in operation for 300 years.

The place is presided over by Netta Bottone. A short, staunch Ravellesi, she runs her establishment with an unyielding if kindly hand. She is the picture of the hard-working Italian matrona, firm if not without irony, who is close to the land, the seasons, the crops, and the vines – to the daily narrative of town gossip, and to ties of blood. She is also a shrewd businesswoman, putting on a show but having the culinary skills to back it up.

We feasted on antipasti, Fettucine Bolognese, and delectable fried seafood. I noticed a picture of Gore Vidal on the wall and asked Netta about him. She gave a knowing grin as if she was recalling earlier times. He ate there often. She said he was a very nice man. There was a certain hushed reverence, something most Ravellesi display whenever his name is mentioned.

It was the same a few days later at Zaccaria in Amalfi, another Vidal haunt. More fritto misto and a seafood scialatelli. Another picture of Gore with friends. The proprietor regaled us, as best he could (his English was as limited as our Italian), with a few anecdotes about "Il Maestro," as they called him, and brought over a photograph of Vidal sitting at the same table.

It is no surprise that Vidal chose the mountains and terraces of Ravello for a place to live and work; it is a dream place and one that has long attracted artistic lodgers. The scenery inspired the second act of Wagner's *Parsifal.* D.H. Lawrence wrote part of *Lady Chatterley's Lover* in Ravello and Andre Gide used the piazza for the opening scenes of *The Immoralist.* All of the Bloomsbury group visited at one time or another, and Forster wrote "The Story of a Panic" during one visit.

Vidal did some of his finest work in Ravello: about the state of literature and civilization, on the danger of sky gods, and on the great subject to which he devoted most of his working life – the United States. Ultimately, Vidal became his country's biographer and conscience, answerable to no one. He adhered to Thucydides' dictum: "We Greeks believe that a man who takes no part in public affairs is not merely lazy, but good for nothing."

In Vidal, stunning good looks combined with enormous talent and a fine lineage. "Gore Vidal has the looks of a prince, the connections of a prince, more wit than any prince I can presently recall, and a prose style that should be the envy of the dwindling few who realize that prose style matters," Larry McMurtry once observed.

Vidal was a rare phenomenon in the second half of the 20th century – a man of the 18th, with an encyclopedic memory. Unlike nearly all of the writers of his generation, he was a novelist of ideas. While his despised contemporaries Mailer and Updike came out of dark Romanticism and small town, conformist Protestantism, Vidal's artistic roots were determined by intellect. He was most deeply influenced by Petronius, Sterne, Swift, and Henry James.

Most novelists write about victims; Vidal was a connoisseur of power, both its uses and abuses. A man of imperial manner, oracular self-assurance, and caustic wit, Vidal had no compunction about skewering the pretensions of the powerful or the sensibilities of the majority. He propounded a populist political line, radical only in its adherence to the spirit of the old Republic.

Vidal hated tyranny, any form of absolutism, and trading American blood for oil; he believed in personal freedom, economic equality and the Bill of Rights. He had high expectations. He talked to people without patronizing them, expecting that they would be as well-read as he was and be able to converse on his terms. That which failed to meet his standards – the follies of the literary scene and the abuses of the ruling class – was savaged with his customary wit. He held a razor, not a mirror, to reality, and this made him somewhat of a man apart.

"The Presidency is the one thing I really wanted. And didn't get," Vidal would admit. He was thwarted by his inability to not tell the truth – or tame his tongue. At heart, he was an educator, and a didactic vein ran through all his novels and essays. Vidal did not write for those who accept life as it is dished out without reflection or thought. A profound humanist, he believed like George Bernard Shaw that society can and should be improved by human intelligence – not a very fashionable view of late. He quoted Logan Pearsall Smith about wanting most "to set a chime of words tinkling in the minds of a few fastidious people." Surely he did.

"I am at heart a propagandist, a tremendous hater, a tiresome nag, complacently positive that there is no human problem which could not be solved if people would simply do as I advise," Vidal wrote early on. He championed the conclusions that his intellect led him to, and didn't care who was offended as he relentlessly exposed hypocrisy and injustice.

His output – twenty-five novels, collections of essays, plays, television scripts and film scripts – was nothing less than Trollopian. I cannot think of any other public intellectual who provided such a profound contribution to our national discourse, or a more realistic portrayal of American society, for as long as Vidal did. If he was not appreciated, it was because Americans tend to see any criticism of their country as mere cynicism.

Yet his public image, that of an *agent provocateur*, which he was all too happy to cultivate on his many lecture tours and TV appearances, had an unfortunate side effect. As Harold Bloom observed, Vidal's substantial body of work remains "vastly underestimated by American academic criticism." It was an unfortunate fate for "the best all-around American man of letters since Edmund Wilson."

Vidal was not to everyone's taste – an elegant stylist with a talent to delight and annoy in equal measure. "It's all because I talk in complete sentences and this is hateful to most people. There are a lot of people who can but won't because it sounds arrogant. So they say 'Isn't he arrogant?' and it's simply because he said 'Yes, I do think it is a nice afternoon, but I do believe it's going to rain'."

Vidal's death this year brought a wave of tributes. In the big media, one could detect a palpable sense of relief: the old nag had finally crossed the shining river. But that could have been expected. It was more disheartening to see his legacy reduced to twitterings of his pithy, caustic quotes. Vidal had often bemoaned the focus on writers' personalities, rather than on their *work*. In death, it was no different: throw-away puff pieces filled with typically American obsessions: the many famous people he had known, his bisexuality, his feuds. They were quite thin on the work, but that was nothing new.

The digital memorial was inapposite, to say the least. Vidal was one of the most analog of men, and one wonders what sarcastic remark he would have made, though I don't doubt he would have loved the attention. Born in an era when linear type still reigned supreme and raised before television emerged, his mind was wired differently. He was a fierce reactionary against our post-Gutenberg world, deploring the replacement of the text with the audio-visual. He wrote essays on a typewriter; novels in longhand, with a fountain pen, on yellow legal paper. He used a fax machine but never a computer.

It was touching to see how many people had been influenced by his work. Some were even incisive. One mourner wrote: "Gore Vidal was our American Cicero. He valiantly stood as our golden shield of republican virtue against the brassy sword of empire yielded by plutocratic militarists and their vulgar plebeians… Something great has gone out of the world with his passing."

This was appropriate. Vidal had been steeped in the classics since his youth, and saw disturbing similarities in the collapse of ancient Rome: an imperfect republic, with certain virtues, turned avaricious, corrupted empire run by mercenaries for the benefit of the propertied elite. Vidal was an aristocrat who turned against the aristocracy once his beliefs were betrayed. "The United States was founded by the brightest people in the country – and we haven't seen them since," he said.

There was a nice quote from novelist Dave Eggers: Vidal "meant everything to me when I was learning how to write and learning how to read. His words, his intellect, his activism, his ability and willingness to always speak up and hold his government accountable, especially, has been so inspiring to me I can't articulate it."

Most of the tributes, without apparent coordination, contained some variant of "He was a man, take him for all in all / I shall not look upon his like again." The pundits knew, not only what the nation had lost, but also what we would never see again in this post-literate age and lowest common denominator culture.

One would have liked to have kept, if only for a little longer, our greatest (last) living man of letters in the present tense.

Eugene Luther Gore Vidal was born on October 3, 1925, at West Point. His father, Gene Vidal, was a former quarterback and Olympic athlete, and would serve as FDR's director of air commerce in the mid-thirties; his mother Nina Gore was a bitchy "virago," a "lush 1920s flapper." It was an unhappy marriage. Nina was unloving, constantly drunk and regularly threatened suicide. "She told me that rage made her orgasmic. I didn't think to ask her if sex did the same," her son recalled. Vidal was ten when Nina said that, and she seems to be the source of his sardonic wit.

Vidal would rid himself of the first two names at the age of fourteen; there was already a Gene and he did not want to be called "junior." Gore loved his father as much as he despised his mother. "We knew each other for 43 years, we agreed on nothing and we never quarreled," he said.

The Vidals were northern, Catholic and recent immigrants; the Gores southern, Protestant and American since the 1690s. He was brought up a Southerner. "From my love for grits and red-eye gravy to an overdeveloped sense of honor – which I was to symbolize dramatically three times on-screen as Billy the Kid – I have always been an odd man out in a society of self-invented hustlers, literary and otherwise."

Gore was a voracious reader from the beginning, a passion instilled by his grandfather, Senator Thomas Pryor Gore of Oklahoma, who he simply called "Dah." His first book is telling: an English translation of Livy, *Tales from Livy*. The classical world, particularly Rome, loomed large from the beginning.

Senator Gore, a grizzled western populist, was an incorruptible man who stood against Wall Street and the vested interests. The senator had been blind from the age of 10, and young Gore escorted him around the Capitol and often read to him: "a great deal of history, law naturally, the *Congressional Record*," he later said. "If I got anything from Dah, it was the ability to detect the false notes in those arias that our shepherds lull their sheep with." When the senator died in 1949 Vidal couldn't bring himself to go to the funeral: "My thanatophobia took over."

As a youth, Vidal was transfixed by Catherine Dale Snedeker's *The Spartan* and the Oz books of L. Frank Baum. In *Glinda of Oz*, the last book, the Supreme Dictator says: 'I'm the Supreme Dictator of all, and I am elected once a year. This is a democracy, you know, where people are allowed to vote for their rulers. A good many would like to be Supreme Dictator, but as I made a law that I am always to count the votes myself, I am always elected.'

Rome, a strain of cynicism (i.e. realism) and an old-style American populism: most of the Vidalian cornerstones were in place.

In 1935 Vidal's mother divorced his father, marrying the financier Hugh Auchincloss, and Gore went to live at Merrywood, his stepfather's estate. Compared to the Athens of his grandfather's house, Merrywood was Sparta – a place without culture or charm. This match would give Gore a stepsister when Auchincloss later married Jackie Kennedy's mother.

Vidal was bored with school, finding little to challenge him. Throughout his adolescence he would read all of Shakespeare, Twain, and Crane; he also developed a great love of movies. At St. Albans, a D.C. private school, he wrote his earliest essays and made his first trip to Europe in 1939. War was looming. He saw the Forum, the Baths of Caracalla, saw Mussolini and smelled the buffoon's acrid perfume from afar. Then on to Phillips Exeter Academy in New Hampshire, where Gore ignored the curriculum and spent most of his time reading and writing essays, poems and a few aborted novels.

Vidal was an autodidact. He made charts to figure out world civilization down the ages – what was going on in Greece, Rome, Egypt and the east at any given time, including the literature, arts, economics, sciences, philosophy and religion. Throughout his life, he would amass a library of approximately 8,000 books.

Most of Vidal's early political opinions came from the old senator, who strongly opposed American involvement in both world wars. Gore joined a debating society at Exeter, founding the school's branch of America First, a group that advocated isolationism. He would retain those views, but later substantially reject his grandfather's domestic views, such as opposition to the New Deal.

The patterns that would guide him for the rest of his life were largely set – a commitment to the general welfare born from the aristocrat's sense of *noblesse oblige*, a love of pre-Christian Europe, high standards and a belief in the importance of literature. Soon he would gain both a disdain for empire and for those fundamentalists who sought to impose Bronze Age morality on sexual practices that he believed were perfectly normal.

Vidal joined the army at 17 and liked to recall the indoctrination sessions where recruits were "taught" to tell the difference between America's "exquisite" Chinese allies and "brutish" Japanese enemies. "The principal difference," the information officer announced, "is the pubic hair. The Japanese is thick and wiry while the Chinese is straight and silky."

"I fear that I alone raised my hand to ask what sly strategies we were to use to determine friend from foe," he later joked.

Vidal served as first mate on a freight supply ship in the Aleutians, contracted rheumatoid arthritis, was sent to Florida, and wrote *Williwaw* as an attempt to make money (both Gene and Senator Gore were self-made). That first novel was written in the sparse prose and straight narrative of Steinbeck and Hemingway. He wrote what he knew about: serving on a ship in the Aleutians. He recalled those early years as a writer as being very difficult: "It was like trying to fence in a straightjacket." He was not yet writing in his own voice.

Sales of *Williwaw* were indifferent, yet Vidal was hailed by critics as one of the "war novelists." Not wanting to spend any more time in institutions he opted not to go to college, and never regretted it. His life would be anything but conventional.

Senator Gore had political plans for his grandson, wanting to set him up with a congressional seat in New Mexico. Vidal later joked that he had to choose between writing and politics. "The writer must always tell the truth, and the politician must never give the game away. These are two conflicting drives." His main goal at the time was to write a bolder novel about the only love affair he had ever had.

At the age of 14, Gore had met Jimmie Trimble at St. Albans. A blue-eyed, blond jock and aspiring baseball star, Trimble was the opposite of the intellectual, introspective Vidal. "His sweat smelled of honey, like that of Alexander the Great." They fell in love and had sex in the forest on the edge of the school grounds.

"It was the first human happiness I had ever encountered." At the age of 19, Jimmie Trimble was killed on Iwo Jima, blown up by a hand grenade and

Japanese suicide attack. "He was like a twin – the other half of me who never grew up."

Gore soon wrote *The City and the Pillar* (1948), a dark, bitter book that imagined how things would have gone if he had met Trimble after the war. In the book, the sex failed, and the protagonist, disillusioned that the relationship was not as he remembered, killed the other boy at the end. It was a bold statement for the time, dealing explicitly with homosexual love. Some were pleased, most were bewildered, and the "respectable" media blacklisted him. The book was a best seller but Orville Prescott of *The New York Times* declared that he would never review another of Vidal's books. It also seemed to doom any hope of electoral office.

"In 1948 *The New York Times* would not advertise it and no major American newspaper or magazine would review it or any other book of mine for the next six years. *Life* magazine thought that the greatest nation in the country, as Spiro Agnew used to say, had been driven queer by the young army first mate they had featured only the previous year, standing before his ship."

After Trimble, Vidal cauterized himself emotionally. "It would be greedy to expect a repetition. I was aware of my once perfect luck and left it at that." Vidal threw himself into sex with more than a thousand youths – no names, no repeat visits, pleasure taken but not reciprocated.

There is a picture of Vidal, looking every inch the *enfant terrible* with Truman Capote and Tennessee Williams, at the Gotham Book Mart. He was a "Luciferian-looking young man who called a couple of times. Very gifted, brilliant, and fixed in facility as I am," Dawn Powell wrote in her diaries. His essays would later resurrect her as a first-rate novelist.

That was during what Vidal later called the "Golden Age," the only time that his country was not at war – large or small, hot or cold – during his lifetime. Between 1945 and 1950, the arts and literature flourished; Gore returned to Rome. Italy was coming back to life after Fascism. The food was cheap, as was the sex. He and Tennessee drove down to the Amalfi Coast in an old jeep and saw Ravello for the first time. "I thought it was the most beautiful place I'd ever seen."

Though his disillusion with romantic love would remain unchanged, Gore met a younger man named Howard Austen on Labor Day 1950. They settled down in the Hudson River Valley and would live together for more than half a century. The secret: it was a friendship; no sex or romance. "Each had a sex life apart from the other: all else including our sovereign, Time, was shared."

Among their closest friends were Paul Newman and Joanne Woodward. "I thought Paul was the most beautiful man I'd ever seen, but when I met Gore I said: 'There are two of them,'" Joanne recalled. "He was gorgeous. I loved that he took me seriously, but he also made fun of me because I was very serious and pretentious as hell. And he didn't allow that. But he also didn't treat me like a dingbat."

Vidal had bought a convent in Guatemala, which he used as a writing retreat to work on *Dark Green, Bright Red* (1950). It was the first American novel to anticipate the country's nefarious involvement in the third world. Four years later Washington overthrew President Arbenz of Guatemala after the latter tried to tax the profits of the United Fruit Company. The book also anticipated one of the major concerns of Vidal's fiction and essays for the next five decades – the need to reassess the nation he had served and chart its progress from republic to empire.

Turning away from the narrow realism of his first few novels, Vidal soon expanded both his horizons and his prose, soaking up the classical European novel and its classical antecedents – *The Satyricon* and *The Golden Ass*. His literary genealogy ran: Petronius,

Juvenal, Apuleius, Shakespeare, Peacock, Meredith, Flaubert, James and Proust. In his seventh novel, *The Judgment of Paris* (1952), Gore found his voice. Though it approached the novel of ideas of Peacock – little action, characters sitting around making brilliant talk – the book was a commercial failure.

Vidal's next book began his long fascination with "the religious instinct in man." In *Messiah* (1954) he envisioned "a world religion based upon a charismatic leader, who was a master of television, a great performer" who was able to convert people to his death cult – Cavesway. He asked: "Since death is nothing, and nothing is no thing, how can death be bad?"

The book was a rich parody of the Jesus Christ story; the new messiah, John Cave, turns the Christian emphasis on the afterlife on its head, creating a religion that glorifies death. After proposing the establishment of suicide centers, Cave leads the way, and like Christ takes leave of the world. The new religion is as puritanical and repressive as the old, but flourishes under Cave's disciples.

Vidal's theme is how mass movements arise from the feelings of boredom and irrelevance that come from living in a mechanized society. "Boredom, finally, is the one monster the race will never conquer

—the monster which will devour us in time," the character Clarissa remarks.

The sales of *Messiah* were as bleak as its message; the subject was unattractive amidst the prosperity of the Eisenhower years. Vidal would prove avant-garde; twenty-six years later Jim Jones would sadly confirm his thesis by persuading over 900 people to kill themselves.

Vidal first became interested in Julian the Apostate, the last pagan emperor of Rome, when he read Gibbon at the age of twenty. Julian's reign coincided with a critical turning point in Western history – the growth and eventual triumph of Christianity. Vidal had identified with Rome since childhood; he agreed with Flaubert: "Just when the gods had ceased to be, and the Christ had not yet come, there was a unique moment in history, between Cicero and Marcus Aurelius, when man stood alone."

The civilized Roman of that time despised Christianity for its hatred of the flesh, and so did Vidal. He studied the fourth century intensively, with the intention of putting the emperor into a novel. Yet in the early fifties, he found that he could not make a living from telling people what they did not want to hear. He was nearly broke.

In 1954 Vidal began to write plays for live television, screenplays for Hollywood and plays for Broadway. He helped to rewrite the script of *Ben-Hur* in 1958, and MGM soon allowed him an early exit from his five-year contract. Vidal continued to make notes for a novel about Julian and wrote the first two chapters in 1959. He halted work to write *The Best Man* (1960), the first Broadway play to offer a realistic view of American politics.

By the end of the fifties, Vidal – an angry, practical utopian – was so far removed from the "two-party" middle that he identified with no party. As his biographer, Fred Kaplan wrote, "He embraced a conservatism so radical that to the conservatives he was no conservative at all. And his radicalism was so conservative, so rational, so much an expression of enlightenment utopianism" that radicals did not accept him either.

"He and I used to have this dream that he would run for president and he would get elected," Joanne Woodward said. "And then we would overthrow the government and he would become the Emperor and I was going to become sort of the Empress. And that we could redo the White House. It was glorious. And he was going to rewrite the Constitution."

In 1960 Vidal threw his hat into the political ring, running for Congress as a Democrat-Liberal in upstate New York's 29th District. Campaigning behind the slogan "You'll Get More with Gore," he advocated increased education spending, a slashed defense budget, and recognition of Communist China.

Vidal lost the traditionally Republican district, but had the best showing of any Democrat in memory, winning 44 percent of the vote. He was proud that he received more votes than his friend Jack Kennedy at the head of the ticket ("he was riding on my coattails"). His politics would remain firmly on the left side of our narrow American spectrum, but those politics would now go into the writing. Between president and writer, he had made his choice, and it would not be without regret.

We are in Trimble's debt for dying, and Gore's for his intent on living well. His work in TV, the theatre and Hollywood was purely mercenary, yet it gave him financial security. He could now turn his attention back to the novel, the essay – to attempts, like Montaigne, to understand everything.

Gore's mother Nina disapproved of Howard, continued to make his life miserable, and he permanently cut ties with her in the late fifties. Mommy dearest may have had a toxic effect on his personality. "What superb and seamless armour he wears, as befits one for whom life is a permanent battle for (social and intellectual) supremacy... Gore could never surrender (i.e., expose) himself to anyone," his old friend Ken Tynan wrote in his diaries.

On a visit to Athens in 1961, Vidal would write the Athenian chapter of what would become *Julian* (1964), one of his best. Wanting to establish himself as a serious artist, and escape the distractions and feuds of the New York literary world, Vidal moved to Rome and re-dedicated himself to work.

Having seen entire generations of its boys decimated in two World Wars, Europe had embraced the truths of that other satirist, de Sade. Four of those constants – eating, fucking, shitting, and dying – were accepted, while killing was minimized as much as possible. The welfare state swept away the imperialist power, and civilization was wrought from chaos and totalitarianism.

Monotheism had been largely abandoned in Italy and Europe, and private sexual behavior remained private – a great attraction to Vidal. Italy was also in the blood. From the late 1500s until 1779 his father's people lived in Forni a Voltri in Friuli. They had moved there from Feldkirch, Austria.

"A Vidal then left Friuli to return to Feldkirch, where he bought back Vidalhaus; it was his son, my great-grandfather, who came to the United States in 1848. We were apothecaries for more than five hundred years, and I suppose that the Vidals in the Veneto who make the soap are remnants of the family who stayed on in Italy."

Mornings at his apartment on the Via Guilia in Rome were spent on the manuscript; afternoons at the gym or the library of the American Academy; evenings with friends in the world of trattorias. There was the added attraction of a multitude of willing, nice Italian boys. "I had never had a proper human-scale village life anywhere on earth until I settled into that old Roman street."

Vidal was a pre-Christian moralist, half-Stoic, half-Epicurean, who believed in the commandments on not killing, stealing, and lying; the rest could be safely discarded. Ironically, those three sins were the pillars upon which the church was built. Vidal made many discoveries while writing *Julian*. Christianity, an anthology of all the old gods and local cults, was largely invented in the fourth century. "At a series of Ecumenical Councils during Julian's lifetime, the

Trinity was invented as well as the Doctrine of the Holy Ghost and the beginning of the Cult of Mary."

The myth of a dying and resurrecting godman, born on Christmas before three shepherds and dying at Easter as a sacrifice for the world's sins, had existed in the Mediterranean for something like 1500 years and goes back to the earliest Egyptian spiritual texts. In Greece, he was Dionysus, in Egypt Osiris, in Persia Mithras. But the god needed a mother. The most powerful deity around the central sea had always been the Great Mother Goddess – whether called Demeter, Isis, Astarte, or Diana of Ephesus. So there was born Mary. If the gods were all the same, merely changing their names, why was Christianity a bad thing? The novel provided an answer.

The "bright pagan world" and its death amidst the rise of Christian absolutism was at the center of *Julian*. The radical difference between Christianity and the old myths was that none of the ancients believed any of those stories were historical. Christians synthesized and then made literal what had been symbolic; it was the first world religion to reject diversity of belief, the first to say "we are absolutely true." This was something new in the ancient world. "Think not that I am come to send peace on earth: I came not to send peace, but a sword" (Matthew 10:34).

Julian (331-363) was the nephew of Emperor Constantine, who made Christianity the state religion. Julian's traumatic childhood saw the murder of his family by his Christian cousin Constantius. As a bookish teenager, Julian began to drift away from his family's faith, and he soon renounced Christianity for various mystery cults. A series of improbable events in his twenties led to his debut in Imperial politics, a glorious military career in Gaul and a sudden rise to the purple. The timely death of his cousin left Julian sole master of the Roman world.

By any standard, the course of Julian's short life is remarkable, dramatic, and tragic. Circumstance forced him to play a series of roles. The orphaned child unsure of his own survival; the dispassionate catechist; the philosopher and devotee of the mysteries; the talented general and administrator; the Emperor; the champion of religious toleration and restorer of the old gods; and the conqueror attempting to repeat the feats of the great Alexander. At the pinnacle of his power, his fortunes and judgment began to desert him. Julian was killed in battle in Persia at the age of 32.

Vidal accurately conveyed Julian's own anti-Christian polemic:

Is one to believe that a thousand generations of men, among them Plato and Homer, are lost because they did not worship a Jew who was supposed to be god? A man not born when the world began? I am afraid it takes extraordinary self-delusion to believe such things.

"He was essentially a pluralist," Vidal said. "He thought that people's religious beliefs should not be State, that they should be individual. If you want to worship Jupiter you can, if you want to worship Jehovah you can. It made no difference. So he set out, not to destroy Christianity, he simply did not want it to be the state religion. Instead, he wanted freedom of religion… '"He will not even allow us to become martyrs!' shouted one angry bishop."

Despite Julian's peculiar religious views and vain attempt to organize all the old mysteries "into one grand Hellenic Church," Vidal found him to be "an engaging and a good man." Vidal did not ignore Julian's faults. Speaking in the voice of Priscus, a Cynic philosopher and friend of the emperor, Vidal demonstrates an understanding of Julian lacking in all his historical biographers:

Poor Julian wanted to believe that man's life is profoundly more significant than it is. His sickness was the sickness of our age. We want so much not to be extinguished at the end that we will go to any length to make conjurer-tricks for one another simply to obscure the bitter, secret knowledge that it is our fate not to be... Julian was Christian in everything except his tolerance of others. He was what the Christians would call a saint. Yet he swung fiercely away from the one religion which suited him perfectly, preferring its eclectic origins, which he then tried to systematize into a new combination quite as ridiculous as the synthesis he had rejected... Why is it so important to continue after death? We never question the demonstrable fact that before birth we did not exist, so why should we fear becoming once more what we were to begin with.

Yet Vidal was optimistic. "Had he lived, there is no doubt that Christianity would have been one of several religions in the West. And this diversity might have saved the world considerable anguish." The emperor's failure was one of the great "what-ifs" of world history.

Christianity won and Julian's successors extinguished the old religions with a ruthlessness that anticipated Stalin. Riotous monks looted and destroyed temples and libraries, robbing their descendants of much of ancient knowledge. Books were burnt or left to crumble to dust. The natural world and Greek rationality were abandoned in favor of unquestioning faith and conquest. The Church would reign for more than a millennium, bringing ignorance, the Crusades, the Inquisition, the massacre of Incas, Aztecs and Maya, and several American presidents who believed "God" was whispering in their ear.

For all of Rome's horrors, it represented the best of mankind. "The Christians, those intellectual barbarians, conquered the civilized and called them pagan and decadent. Our problem today is that we are the children of the barbarians, not the civilized."

Julian was a great success and rose to the top of *The New York Times* bestseller list. The novel was Vidal's attack against the absolutist temperament that the emperor hated – and the most visible symptom of civilization's decline in our own time.

Vidal would spend the bulk of each year in Italy for the next forty years, moving to a penthouse on the top of the gray and mustard-colored Origo Palace at the corner of Corso Vittorio Emanuele and Via di Torre Argentina. The area around the Largo Argentina was thick with truncated pillars, ruined columns, cypress, pine and populated by hordes of cats. Why did he want to live in Rome? Vidal was asked during his appearance in Fellini's *Roma* (1972)

First of all, because I like the Romans. They don't give a damn whether you're dead or alive. They're neutral, like the cats. Rome is the city of illusions. Not only by chance, you have here the church, the government, the cinema. They each produce illusions...like you do and like I do. We're getting closer and closer to the end of the world because of too many people. Too many cars, poisons. And what better city than Rome which has been reborn so often? What place could be more peaceful...It's the ideal city for waiting to see if it will really come to an end or not.

Vidal's growing fears about overpopulation and pollution, and his walks through the city with all its neutered statues, soon gave him the idea for a novel about a Malthusian vixen who believed "in breaking the phallus, not for prudish reasons, but as a means of birth control."

Myra Breckinridge, Vidal's most controversial novel, was written in one spasm between new moon and new moon, April to May 1967, and then was much rewritten. A sequel, *Myron* (1974), came later. They were the first of what Vidal called his "inventions" – funny, satiric flights of fancy; not always successful, but the books he most enjoyed writing.

Myra/Myron tells the story of a man called Myron who undergoes a sex-change operation and becomes Myra, takes over a movie studio, and rapes her film idol with a dildo. The heterosexual man was converted to full-blown homosexuality after one passive session of intercourse. Myra/Myron is unbalanced, schizophrenic – the man-hating woman vs. the gay man in the closet. The sex change is destabilized after Myra is hit by a car. The two find themselves trapped in a 1940s movie and battle over the body. Myron wins, getting his body back permanently.

"I will sign off by saying that the highly articulately

silent majority to which I am darned proud to belong are happy with things as they are and that we are not going to let anybody, repeat *anybody*, change things from what they are," Myron says.

The two novels are Vidal's response to the boring, homogenous fifties – suburbs, one man with one woman, heterosexual sex, consumerism; a witty attack on Judeo-Christian moral puritanism and the damage it does to the human condition. At its core is Vidal's contention that a puritanical, repressed country has the potential to descend into a self-destructive hatred of maleness.

He always argued that "there is no such thing as a homosexual person, any more than there is such a thing as a heterosexual person. The words are adjectives describing sexual acts, not people. The sexual acts are entirely normal; if they were not, no one would perform them."

Myra was a great success and made Vidal very rich. Many did not get the point, calling it "jejune pornography." Those who thought they were buying literary porn were disappointed; the book is not the least bit titillating. Its antecedents in the classical world were Petronius' *The Satyricon* and, in turn, Plato's *The Symposium*. This was lost on nearly all

American reviewers; Vidal was pleased that the British ones noticed it.

Vidal had his most dramatic public moment in August 1968 at the Democratic Convention in Chicago. He had agreed to a series of debates on ABC with the conservative pundit William F. Buckley, Jr. Buckley was disdainful, attacking Gore's "perverted, Hollywood-minded prose" and Vidal, politely condescending, calling him the "Marie Antoinette of the right-wing" with "blood-thirsty neuroses." But the nonplussed, smiling Vidal, who spoke a great deal less than his opponent, clearly won the debates.

When protestors were brutally attacked by the Chicago police, Buckley attacked those who spoke against the war in Vietnam.

Gore responded: "If you're going to have freedom of assembly and freedom of speech you must be able to say it. That is the whole point of this country, and once this is abrogated then I think we might just as well stop these wars of freedom. What are we doing fighting in Vietnam if you cannot freely express yourself in the streets of Chicago?"

Their long-standing antagonism erupted on August 28, when Buckley compared the opponents of the war to Nazi appeasers. Vidal said, "The only pro or crypto-Nazi I can think of is yourself." Buckley quivered and shot back: "Listen you queer stop calling me a crypto-Nazi or I'll sock you in the goddamn face and you'll stay plastered."

Buckley's crudeness highlighted all that Gore thought was wrong with perceptions of sex in America. So much for trying to raise the level of discourse on television, and with someone entirely bereft of intellectual nuance.

Vidal had liked Jack Kennedy ("the President-erect") tremendously. They both had voracious sexual appetites. "Jack was fun" yet "one of the most disastrous presidents" for his substantial commitment to Vietnam. Lyndon Johnson (the "corn pone Genghis Khan") then attempted the conquest of Asia. Vidal had become so repulsed by the war that he believed the most patriotic thing he could do would be to change nationality. He found property in West Cork, Ireland. Having Irish ancestors on both sides (the Anglo-Irish Gores had come from County Donegal in the 17th century) would facilitate citizenship, but the scheme never got off the ground.

Vidal had become one of the few serious writers whose name was recognized in both America and

Europe – thanks to both his books and his regular appearances on talk shows like Carson and Cavett. Vidal was naturally detached and remote, and he accentuated those qualities to avoid detracting from his work. "Since we live in a time where the personality of the writer is everything and what he writes is nothing, only a fool would aid the enemy by helping to trivialize his works."

Yet America, both highbrow and low, was unprepared for the sharpness of Vidal's wit and the seemingly malignant intent of his polemics. His image – that of a glib, contemptuous patrician, confused some and infuriated others. To both critics and the *vox populi* "what matters is not if a book is good or bad (who, after all, would know the difference?) but whether or not the author is a good person or bad person." Since his character was suspect, the attention that should have been directed toward his work was directed at him, and his personal life.

To Vidal it was clear why he was resented: he was a truth-teller and "Americans prefer their serious writers obscure, poor, and, if possible, doomed by drink or gaudy vice." He could lay claim to none of these things. Moreover, his satire cut deep, revealing how far we have fallen from the ideal.

The television barbs, pronounced in his mellifluous, high-WASP voice, were nothing if not entertaining. On Jack Kennedy: "We always said Jack would do for sex what Eisenhower had done for golf." Or Truman Capote: "A Republican housewife from Kansas." Richard Nixon: "He could strangle Pat to death on the television and they would say, 'No she was having a heart attack and he was holding her up by the neck.'" Ted Kennedy: "Every country should have at least one King Farouk." Did Vidal support corporal punishment: "Only between consenting adults." Was his first sexual experience heterosexual or homosexual: "I was too polite to ask."

Vidal loved to cast pebbles and watch the waves they caused. Most of those who were infuriated were simply slow.

Gore felt confined in New York, and then in Rome, and soon expressed a wish for an Italian country home. In late 1971 Howard found a classified ad for a villa in Ravello on the Amalfi Coast. Gore and Howard drove down the peninsula in their old Jaguar to see the house, called La Rondinaia. From the Piazza Duomo they walked to a gate at the back of one of the hotels, passed through several gates to a cliffside path with dazzling views of the Bay of

Salerno, reached a garden and a walkway of cedars and cypress, and passed down steep steers and along another path to the villa itself.

La Rondinaia, a Saracen style place of five levels, was built into the side of the stone cliff and equipped with a profusion of balconies and terraces. The property came with several agricultural terraces for lemon and olive trees. The price was $272,000. By the time Gore walked down the cypress allée, he knew he wanted the house (built "like me" he would joke, in 1925). He could pay cash and the property was his by early 1972.

Gore had come to depend on Howard to run their domestic affairs; Howard was the more social of the two and dealt with bills, practical matters, and parties. Gore's critics portrayed him as a social butterfly, who attended too many parties and knew too many celebrities. He had great fun, of course, availing himself of all the sensual pleasures life offered. Vidal played the *grand seigneur* well and enjoyed it. He had many famous guests, including Paul Newman and Joanne Woodward, Mick Jagger, Claire Bloom, and Princess Margaret.

Yet many of his friends, whether in Rome or Ravello, noticed that he spent much of his day in his study, and even snuck out during parties to make note of something that popped into his head. "Henry James and Edith Wharton led far more active social lives and it never harmed their work," he once said.

Vidal was a meticulous researcher and his tremendous output, in a multitude of styles and genres, would not have been possible without his sense of discipline. His routine was sacred: hung-over or not he was up by 10 or 10:30 and had a cup of coffee; he would read proofs or write, eat a simple lunch, and work until mid-afternoon. Then he would walk down to Amalfi for the papers, take the bus back, answer mail and work out. After another hour or so of more work, he would drink and have dinner around nine, either alone with Howard, or out at restaurants with a few friends. He would stay up reading or chatting with guests, until 2 or 3 in the morning.

Vidal began to reinvent himself as his country's biographer. His novel *Washington D.C.* (1967), which came between *Julian* and *Myra*, had attempted to capture the city during the era of FDR. It is compelling and reads well, but Gore felt that he had "bungled the job," failing to render "the wheel as it turns in the night, the sense of a republic becoming an empire."

"My own impression of the book," he wrote his cousin Louis Auchincloss, "is that it is unexpectedly sad, and I can't think why. My own contempt for empire has always been…complete but cheerful. Instead I am as gloomy as Tacitus without ever being able for one moment to believe, as he did, that the Republic was much better."

By the end of the sixties, Vidal had amassed a considerable library of books and documents about Aaron Burr, Jr., one of America's "forgotten founders." *Burr* was begun in Rome and finished the year he bought La Rondinaia. It took years of research and took Gore back to the founding of the Republic. The Founders were not saints, and he portrayed them with both their warts and flashes of brilliance.

Every story needs a villain (or a scapegoat) and the Revolutionary generation had Burr. His lineage – the grandson of the Calvinist firebrand Jonathan Edwards – was impeccable. Burr was one of the most unquestionably aristocratic of all the Founders and the "boy hero" of Quebec, who served ably in war and quickly became a political power in the new country.

Burr was a Chesterfieldian gentleman, very intelligent and something of a rascal, which largely explains why Vidal fancied him. Unlike the other Founders, Burr found no need to reiterate a belief in public welfare. Unlike Hamilton he avoided conflict, and unlike Jefferson he was not a hypocrite. Like both he had a penchant for fine things and amassed great debts; unlike them, he had no ideology. For Burr politics was "fun, honor and profit," which made him a threat to his two zealous rivals.

Burr was effectively America's first professional politician – hardly the "disinterested" man that the others felt could properly look after the public good. Burr had set up what would become Tammany Hall and quickly became the preeminent power in New York. He enrolled new immigrants in tenements and set up a bank for them. They had a base, from which they could vote, and Burr soon controlled New York and a great deal of New England.

Burr's political views were pragmatic; though nominally a Republican, he flirted at times with the Federalists. He doubted that the Constitution would last fifty years, which of course it would not, due to amendments. Unlike Jefferson, Burr had a high opinion of women, rejecting the Calvinist purities of his grandfather and educating his daughter Theodosia as if she were a son. He believed blacks should be made a part of the mainstream of society and was against Indian removal. Burr was in favor of a looser Federal structure and thought that Jefferson's idea of Nullification set a dangerous precedent. He ardently believed in free speech and the right to trial by jury – the pillars of our system. In short, Burr was the perfect Vidalian avatar.

Burr's influence was such that Jefferson needed him even while plotting to do him in. Burr's tragedy was that he was "no fool but easily fooled by others." Before the election of 1800, a bargain was struck: Jefferson would be president; Burr would be vice president and succeed Jefferson. In return, Burr would deliver New York's electoral votes for the Republicans. The two men unexpectedly tied – with seventy-three votes apiece – and the election was thrown into the House of Representatives.

Hamilton attacked Burr as an "embryo-Caesar;" many Federalists were determined to support Burr over Jefferson, whom they saw as the American Robespierre. Burr refused to break his word and did not fight for the presidency. Yet he earned Jefferson's lasting animus. With help from Hamilton, Jefferson emerged victorious; the throne of sorts he had long suspected the "monarchist" Hamilton of seeking was now his.

As vice president, Burr found himself sidelined as Jefferson maneuvered to position a Virginian to succeed. With rivals conspiring to drive him out of New York politics, Burr returned to rebuild his power base. Backed by a group of Federalists who wanted New York and New England to secede from the Union, Burr ran for governor in 1804. Hamilton's opposition led to Burr's defeat and the famous duel at Weehawken (Vidal believed that Hamilton had alleged Burr had incestuous relations with his daughter). Their tragedy was almost Shakespearean, in that neither man could put aside their quarrel to unite in the face of their common enemy – Jefferson.

Burr traveled to the west, intending to invade Mexico, kick out the Spanish government, crown himself king, and found the utopia he believed would never flourish on American soil. Burr claimed that Jefferson had tacitly approved the liberation of Mexico; nonetheless, the president had Burr arrested for treason and accused him of trying to separate the West from the Union. There was no evidence, and though Jefferson suborned witnesses, Burr was acquitted.

Burr, which Vidal once said was his favorite of the novels, made the point that empire was implicit from America's beginnings. "Every ambitious man of the period saw himself conquering the earth, like Bonaparte. Both Hamilton and Burr wanted to conquer Mexico, Cuba, South America – simply for the fun of conquest and delights of a crown."

Burr would spend the last years of his long life practicing law in New York City. "Had I read Voltaire less and Sterne more, I might have thought the world wide enough for Hamilton and me," he said.

Burr made Vidal a household name in America. "My God, what a lucky life, I do exactly what I want to do," he said at the time. CBS *60 Minutes*, with its nine-minute "in-depth" features, followed him in Rome and Ravello in 1975 to offer their own assessment of the "gloomy scold." Gore's problem, the problem of every satirist in trying to transform their society, was that he was seen as unrealistically pessimistic.

"I don't seem to be cynical to myself but how what I say goes down with others is their problem. I'm realistic. Come to me and show me a small cancer and I'll tell you you've got a small cancer that should be cut out. That's realism but in America it's called cynicism. You're supposed to say, ah, you've got a little beauty blemish here and I have some marvelous Max Factor that will hide it. That's the American way of handling things. Anyway, I'm a diagnostician not a cosmetician."

The *60 Minutes* piece is illustrative of how television contributes little or nothing toward understanding anything. A few months before the interview, in an essay called "State of the Union" Gore had written:

"There is only one party in the United States, the Property Party...and it has two right wings: Republican and Democrat. Republicans are a bit stupider, more rigid, more doctrinaire in their laissez-faire capitalism than the Democrats, who are cuter, prettier, a bit more corrupt – until recently...and more willing than the Republicans to make small adjustments when the poor, the black, the anti-imperialists get out of hand. But, essentially, there is no difference between the two parties."

That skewering of the American two-party system would have been interesting to talk about, as would have the revisionist account of the Founders Gore had provided in *Burr*.

No such luck. After Gore denounced Kennedy and Johnson for the misadventure in Vietnam, Mike Wallace asked: "What is your current relationship with Mrs. Onassis." Gore was polite: "Haven't seen her since 1962. There was no reason for our lives to cross. She was devoted to Bobby Kennedy, and I, as you know, was plainly not…I kind of like her though, she is very bright, unlike most of the family…She had no interest in anything but herself, which is alright; I mean that's her character. But it is not noble."

The interview begins innocuously enough, then gets silly. Wallace, on behalf of his corporate paymasters, produced a hatchet piece – though an oddly disjointed one. Vidal "hawked" his books (actually Gore usually talked of other subjects on talk shows) and lived in his clifftop "Berchtesgaden" where he wrote and acted as "dilettante anthropologist" and "intellectual vaudevillian."

Hey Mike, how about a question about *1876*? – the novel Vidal was working on for the bicentennial about the centennial, the "dead center of the county."

Wallace is after other game. "Love? Gore," he solemnly intones.

"I don't like the word love, it's like patriotism, it's like the flag, it's the last refuge of scoundrels. When people start talking about what wonderful, warm, deep emotions they have…I watch out, somebody's going to steal something. Romantic love as Americans conceive it does not exist, hence the enormous divorce rate."

WALLACE: You've lived with a man for 23-24 years?

VIDAL: Yes.

WALLACE: You have never been in love with him, nor are now? You are simply good companions? I'm not sure that I understand.

VIDAL: Well, haven't I proved it by living with somebody for 24 years? That's obviously not being in love...

WALLACE: You have sexual congress, if you will, with an assortment of friends?

VIDAL: Whether you will! Oh, well, certainly, I'm devoted to promiscuity, and always have been. I believe the more you do, the better it is for you. I'm a great health nut, and sex is, I think, absolutely marvelous for the whole system; tones you up.

The CBS piece descended into an attack on Gore "the expatriate," who was leaving the "provincial folks" at home to their dark fate. The word "expatriate" has always had a dirty place in the national vocabulary. Vidal didn't think of himself as an expatriate but as a long-term vacationer who came home for business visits. Life in Italy was appealing both emotionally and culturally. His distance from America kept him from descending into anger and helped him hone his perspective. After all, though he had fallen out of love with America, "I don't write about anything other than the fact of being an American."

Vidal liked both Italy and Italians – the "salt of the earth." "Left to themselves, the Italians work out a fine balance between anarchy and order. When times are bad – or good – the balance shifts this way or that. But the nice balance, sooner or later, is restored. Fundamentally, Italians hate both anarchy and order. This is very human."

In 1976, to escape new Italian tax laws, Vidal began to spend more than half the year outside Italy. He bought a Spanish-style house in the high canyons of the Hollywood Hills. The next year he and Howard began summering in Italy and wintering in California.

His life in Italy did not obscure the fact that it was a "Bonaparte-style democracy," where ID cards had to be carried by all. This was alien to American tradition yet increasing becoming a fact of life in his native land. That year, with the declassification of National Security Council Report 68 (NSC-68), Gore began to put what he called "the National Security State" together in his mind. Approved by President Truman in 1950-51, NSC-68 established the blueprint for America's post-war empire and, indeed, a new kind of country. But we will come to all that later.

In the wake of Vietnam, Watergate and the Energy Crisis a deep gloom entered into Vidal's work. He had long feared that the audiovisual was replacing the written word; since Gutenberg knowledge had been "a kinetic operation between the eye and the text." Despite his own sales, the novel was in decline, either unread by the TV-watching masses or ruined by ambitious English teachers unduly concerned with form and innovation. He wrote:

> In any case, rather like priests who have forgotten the meaning of the prayers they chant, we shall go on for quite a long time talking of books and writing books, pretending all the while not to notice that the church is empty and the parishioners have gone elsewhere to attend other gods, perhaps in silence or with new words.

A deep concern with overpopulation and pollution, war and poverty, led Vidal to notice "a sense of an ending" pervading the post-Vietnam world – a sense of hopelessness born from feelings of human irrelevance. His novels during this period were darker than usual.

Kalki (1978), like its predecessor *Messiah*, is the story of another religious leader, a former Vietnam GI and drug entrepreneur in Kathmandu who comes to believe he is Kalki, the tenth incarnation of the god Vishnu. According to Hindu tradition, the tenth would be a white man whose coming would signal the end of the age of Kali and the beginning of a new cycle of creation. "Kalki" becomes very popular on TV, is interviewed on *60 Minutes*, and becomes a celebrity. Yet he continues to warn that everyone will die. On April 3rd this is brought about; the bacteria *Yersinia enterocolitica* is spread throughout the world and only Kalki and four others survive. They will sire the new human race. Ironically, they cannot do so because of incompatible blood types. The species dies and Kalki bequeaths the Earth to two surviving monkeys.

In his next novel, *Creation* (1981), Vidal went back to the 5th century BC and "the origins of all our systems of thought." He began to believe that, much like DNA, the human race was programmed for certain developments. More or less simultaneously in Greece, Persia, China and India "people were developing writing and logical systems of thought and

54

new ethical orientations; they were revolting against a warrior caste that had taken power as invaders from the north; they were turning away from the sky gods who had dominated their cultures in the past."

Once viewing humanity as open-ended, Vidal had begun to think of the species as a "very large virus, with a pre-established life span...A virus can live just so long in a host." Pollution was killing the planet, and with mankind's creation of atomic weapons, Vidal wondered whether "the certainty of destroying ourselves [was] built into mankind from its origins."

Creation is a crash course in comparative religion. Vidal's half-Greek, half-Persian narrator, Cyrus Spitama is a grandson of Zoroaster. He travels the known world on behalf of the Persian ruler and seeks answers about the "only important subject there is" – the creation of the universe. Trying to reconcile his monotheism with the existence of evil, he asks the various wise men he meets: "Who created the Wise Lord? Can the Creator create himself? Why was Evil created along with Good?"

The Jains – Mahavira and Gosala – say the question about creation is false: they don't believe in time. The Buddha says there is no need to know; Laozi, the Taoist preacher says, "I do not know whose child it is;" and Confucius has no interest in how the world was created, or for what purpose.

Cyrus comes to realize he was asking the wrong questions, and that religion cannot explain creation. The materialism of Confucius and Democritus wins the day; after a long life, the latter can report on the causes of creation:

The first principles of the universe are atoms and empty space; everything else is merely human thought. Worlds such as this one are unlimited in number. They come into being, and perish. But nothing can come into being from that which is not, or pass away into what is not. Further, the essential atoms are without limit in size and number and they make of the universe a vortex in which all composite things are generated – fire, water, air, earth...As Cyrus Spitama was beginning to suspect, if not believe, there is neither a beginning nor an end to a creation which exists in a state of flux in a time that is truly infinite. Although I have nowhere observed the slightest trace of Zoroaster's Wise Lord, he might well be a concept which can be translated into that circle which stands for the cosmos, for the primal unity, for creation.

Vidal's six-year study of Buddhism, Jainism, Zoroastrianism, Taoism and Confucianism left him what he had been all along: a Confucian who rejected sky gods. "I agree with Confucius that heaven is far and man is near and the proper organizing of society is all-important."

The long project also left Vidal, then 55, with the belief that his ability to work was breaking down. Bored with fiction, he turned increasingly to the essay. Many of his best essays were written while he was researching and writing *Creation* – pieces on the Italian writers Calvino and Sciascia (two writers he introduced to the reading public), on Baum's Oz Books, Thomas Love Peacock, Edmund Wilson, and "Sex Is Politics." A collection of many of these essays, *The Second American Revolution*, was released in 1982, with the title essay providing a survey of the Republic's plight and a series of radically practical reforms.

Vidal could not *not* work hard ("I find that when I do not write, I do not think"). He agreed to do a teleplay for NBC about Abraham Lincoln, which soon grew into the novel that would be his magnum opus and most successful book. Work was fueled by coffee ("This stuff has killed more writers than liquor") and a desire to stave off the melancholy of middle age. So he kept busy ("The mind that doesn't nourish itself devours itself").

By now he had begun to see his original American trilogy as part of a larger chronicle of the exercise of power in the country and the growth of the American Empire. What Gore called his *Narratives of Empire*, would grow into a thirty-year project and provide a long-overdue revisionist account of American history and politics. These "novelized histories" were *Burr* (1973), *1876* (1976), *Lincoln* (1984), *Empire* (1987), *Hollywood* (1990), and *The Golden Age* (2000).

Here is Vidal, a member of the ruling WASP elite, haughtily and grandly giving the game away – exposing how power is exercised and gleefully betraying his class. As the reader will see from the following, Vidal's story is not the idealized narrative of a democratic "shining city," but the nation's actual story – the many vs. the privileged few; an imperfect republic reaching for empire.

2

Until 1788 the Republic was a loose confederation; thirteen autonomous states uneasily bound together by the Articles of Confederation. Many of the states were broke, and it seemed that the young nation would never be able to pay off its enormous war debts. The South feared that a stronger Union would mean the tyranny of New England. George Washington was worried, writing John Jay that "something must be done, or the fabric must fall, for it is certainly tottering." He believed that a stronger central government was essential.

Then Captain Daniel Shays revolutionized Massachusetts. After the war the property qualifications necessary to vote were doubled; Shays did not want London replaced by New York and advocated an abolition of debts and division of property. "The property of the United States has been protected from the confiscation of Britain by the joint exertion of all, and ought to be the common property of all." The rebellion was quickly crushed, but the men of property, led by Washington, were shaken. The general soon emerged from private life. "Influence is no government. Let us have one by which our lives, liberties, and properties will be secured," he wrote Harry Lee.

On the behalf of Washington, and the other land speculators, rumrunners, and slaveholders that we call the "Founders," his protégés Madison and Hamilton devised a Constitution that would make it impossible for a future Shays to lead the indebted masses against the propertied elite.

The Founders hated majoritarian rule as much as monarchy, and so decided that we would be a republic, modeled on pre-Caesarian Rome and governed by a ruling class.

Here is Hamilton on the subject:

All communities divide themselves into the few and the many. The first are rich and well born; the other, the mass of the people. The voice of the people has been said to be the voice of God; and however generally this maxim has been quoted and believed, it is not true in fact. The people are turbulent and changing; they seldom judge or determine right. Give therefore to the first class a distinct, permanent share in the government. They will check the unsteadiness of the second; and as they cannot receive any advantage by change, they will therefore maintain good government.

In September 1787 the Constitutional Convention in Philadelphia finished its work. A three-part republic was created, modeled on the British system: a legislature composed of a Senate and a House of Representatives; a judiciary headed by the Supreme Court, with a less than clearly defined role; and, atop the heap, a president (another King George would have looked bad), who would also act as commander in chief. The franchise was limited to 700,000 propertied adult males.

An Electoral College, composed of the rulers' surrogates to thwart majority rule, was devised to be the ultimate arbiter of presidential elections. Slavery was approved implicitly to keep the South on board. In the First Congress, ten amendments devised by George Mason – the Bill of Rights – were added as an afterthought. They would be regularly violated.

The structure had so many checks and balances

that radical change would be nearly impossible. A Caesar would not be able to usurp it with ease, much less a mob.

The Founders were not terribly proud of their work: Hamilton would later call the Constitution "a worthless fabric;" Jefferson and Adams both disliked that the president could serve multiple terms. But both thought that any faults could be corrected at another convention (we are still waiting).

Benjamin Franklin was far harsher, and prescient:

I agree to this Constitution with all its faults, if they are such; because I think a general Government necessary for us, and there is no form of Government but what may be a blessing to the people if well administered, and believe farther that this is likely to be well administered for a course of years, and can only end in Despotism, as other Forms have done before it, when the People shall become so corrupted as to need Despotic Government, being incapable of any other.

The corruption Franklin feared came rather quickly. Political factions soon developed. Hamilton, the leader of the new city aristocracy who favored a strong central government (later called Federalists), effectively ruled the country during Washington's presidency. He was opposed by Jefferson and Madison, the leaders of those rural magnates who wanted the states to be loosely affiliated (later called Republicans).

The idealistic, naïve Jefferson envisioned (at least early on) a rural arcadia of yeomen farmers with a government composed of little more than a few judges, police and a postal service. Small government would protect the rights of slaveholders. He fought capitalism and modernity, at least initially; as president he would expand the empire of slavery, while his successors would drive the Indians ever westward.

Hamilton, on the other hand, envisioned (and achieved) the creation of a modern capitalist economy and energetic government and executive that required all those things Jefferson didn't want – banks, manufactories, cities, and taxes.

Both, Vidal noted, were "men of extraordinary brilliance" – "each was a sort of monster driven by vanity, but each was also an intellectual philosopher of government, and each thought he was creating a perfect or perfectible system of government."

In 1790 Congress was split over the issue of assumption of the state's debts by the federal government. As Secretary of the Treasury, Hamilton planned to pay off the debt at par. Speculators purchased seemingly worthless securities from unwitting humble investors for pennies on the dollar. They anticipated huge profits when Hamilton bought back the paper at par. States with large debts were willing, while those with small opposed the plan. Hamilton's measures could not get through the House. For a time Jefferson feared that the Union might "burst, and vanish."

In a deal with Jefferson in June to allow the assumption legislation to pass, an "anodyne" was offered to the Southern states (read Virginia) in the form of a new capital on the Potomac. By corrupting the legislature by making them new-rich, Hamilton has secured majorities in the House and Senate. As a more permanent "engine of influence," Hamilton went on to create the extra-constitutional Bank of the United States the following year. Hamilton's fiscal system flourished and the country began to divide into parties.

It was the first corrupt compromise. In 1792 the French minister, Fauchet, penned the following gem:

What will be the old age of this government, if it is thus early decrepit! Such, Citizen, is the evident consequence of the system of finances conceived by Mr. Hamilton. He has made a whole nation of stock-jobbing, speculating, selfish people. Riches alone here fix consideration.

In the presidential election of 1800, the Hamiltonian view of a stronger Federal government was rejected by voters. Jefferson became the third president, and by his second term had become as Hamiltonian as his rival. Gone was the pretense of a farmer's utopia, small government and minimal taxes. Now Jefferson wanted a more activist government, using taxes to build roads and canals and to fund manufacturing, education, and war. What was responsible for the change? Jefferson had launched the nation upon empire, from which it has never looked back.

In 1803 Jefferson subverted the Constitution by buying Louisiana from Napoleon, adding what are now states from Arkansas to the Dakotas to the territory of the United States, and acquiring the citizens of those areas without their consent. He then began efforts to acquire the Floridas. "The apostle of liberty" used the army to enforce laws in time of peace, trampled on the Fourth Amendment (illegal search and seizure), went after editors, and tried on two occasions to break the Supreme Court.

The Republic would remain a fairly loose affair until the Civil War. By the 1820s the interests of the founding elite (John Quincy Adams) clashed with those of the pioneers moving west (Andrew Jackson). Jackson's filibusters into the Spanish Floridas, and the accompanying bloodshed, appealed to the electorate; as did his championing of cheap money to protect indebted farmers.

As secretary of state, Quincy Adams helped draft the Monroe Doctrine, stating that Europe may not interfere in the Western hemisphere and America would not interfere in Europe. The Caribbean and South America were added to the American sphere of influence. The Adams presidency proved disastrous. He was too elite, too intelligent for his time, and caught up in a shift to popular democracy he did not understand (all white men over 21 could now vote). Jackson was the symbol of a new era. His slogan, "Jackson who can fight, and Adams who can write," suggested something else: the republic defined by words as deeds was done. As was the rule of the best and brightest.

Jackson, the champion of the settlers, crushed Adams in the election of 1828. He, like Jefferson, advocated an "agricultural republic." He instituted the spoils system, in which federal employees were replaced with party loyalists. Jackson's destruction of the Second Bank of the United States was, if only for a time, a blow to the elite entrepreneurs.

Nonetheless, the precarious balance between the old big-money Federalists and small-farm, small-government Republicans had been broken. Jackson's policies resulted in the settlement of the center of the continent. In what amounted to ethnic cleansing, the Indians were driven west of the Mississippi or slaughtered. Raw power, land and money had become the principal concerns. While Jackson catered to the mob, Adams, now a congressman, wrote of the president's brutal treatment of the Indians: "These are crying sins for which we are answerable before a higher Jurisdiction."

When the multitude of settlers dwindled to the landless few, exploited by the wealthy fewer, Abraham Lincoln's 1862 Homestead Act opened more western land for settlers – and the opportunity for the elite to separate them from it. Slavery could not be contained. The Missouri Compromise of 1820

allowed slavery to extend south of the parallel 36°30'
north; lands north of the line would be free territory.
People in the North were encouraged to return
runaway slaves.

With mounting tension between the mercantile
North and agricultural South, John C. Calhoun of
South Carolina disinterred Jefferson's old arguments
about states' rights and put them to use on behalf of
the Southern barons.

In response to the Alien-Sedition Acts of 1798 –
an all-out assault on the Bill of Rights, specifically the
First Amendment – Jefferson had secretly proposed
that the states could nullify unconstitutional federal
laws. If the states did not have the right to nullify
tyrannous acts, they should leave the Union. The
secessionist South used Jefferson's logic in 1860, not
in response to an elimination of the First Amendment
(that would have justified rebellion), but rather to
hold on to slavery – an institution directly opposed to
"all men are created equal," endowed "with certain
inalienable rights."

The great contradiction was held at bay under
Jefferson and Jackson, but it could not be contained
forever. No one was more responsible for increasing
the spread of empire and bolstering the pro-slavery
faction, than President James K. Polk. The yeomen

needed more land to be opened up. Aaron Burr's southwest schemes were now in vogue.

Polk annexed Texas, provoking a war with Mexico in 1846. Two years later Mexico ceded California, Nevada, Utah, most of Arizona, and parts of New Mexico, Colorado and Wyoming. In treaties with England Polk acquired Oregon, Washington, and Idaho. The United States now extended from Atlantic to Pacific. U.S. Grant, then a lieutenant, later wrote: "The Southern rebellion was largely the outgrowth of the Mexican war. Nations, like individuals, are punished for their transgressions. We got our punishment in the most sanguinary and expensive war of modern times."

The Supreme Court, a group of life appointees, had been busy since the Republic's founding, proving to be the "wild card in the federal apparatus," in the words of Vidal. Chief Justice John Marshall, who served from 1801 to1835, was another key inventor of the nation.

Marbury v. Madison (1803) established the principle of judicial review, allowing the Court to void the laws of Congress and decrees of presidents – a power *not* granted it by the Constitution. *Dartmouth College v. Woodward* (1819) held that "a corporation is an artificial being, invisible, intangible, and existing only in contemplation of law." This was the keystone of modern conservatism and resulted in the rise of the American corporation.

In *Barron v. City of Baltimore* (1833) the court ruled that the Bill of Rights applied only to the federal government, not the state governments. This ridiculous ruling led to over a century of illegal searches, seizures, detentions, and beatings of individuals by local officials and police. Despite the Fourteenth Amendment (1868), the Bill of Rights was not applied to the states until the 1930s.

The court had usurped powers it had never been granted, and Marshall's heirs helped to make the Civil War inevitable in *Dred Scott v. Sandford* (1857). To return Scott to his "master" the Court declared unconstitutional the Missouri Compromise.

The collection of disparate and squabbling states had held together tenuously for more than seventy years. From 1861 to Appomattox it was preserved at bayonet point and by the sheer will of its greatest president. Abraham Lincoln is a figure who is easy to disagree with but impossible to dislike. He was born poor. He read little, but read and reread Shakespeare. His favorite play was *Macbeth* ("I am in blood.

Stepped in so far that, should I wade no more"). He knew all the guilt speeches. He went on to become a well-to-do railroad lawyer and America's second greatest prose writer. A cold, reflective man and brilliant politician, Lincoln was driven by fiery ambition. At the age of 28, Lincoln, in the voice of Caesar, warned us about Lincoln:

> It is to deny what the history of the world tells us is true to suppose that men of ambitions and talents will not continue to spring up among us…The question then is, can that gratification be found in supporting and maintaining an edifice that has been erected by others? Most certainly it cannot…Towering genius disdains a beaten path. It seeks regions hitherto unexplored…It scorns to tread in the footsteps of any predecessor, however illustrious. It thirsts and burns for distinction; and, if possible, it will have it, whether at the expense of emancipating slaves, or enslaving freemen.

Lincoln was elected in 1860 and the Southern states began to secede, one by one, as was their right under the Constitution (as a congressman Lincoln admitted as much). Lincoln should have freed the South (those "mosquito republics" as Seward called them), just as the South should have freed the slaves. Instead, Lincoln sidestepped the slavery issue by saying that he was charged with the preservation of an indivisible, compulsory Union. The Union – a mystical concept that existed largely in his own mind – was paramount and had to be preserved, at any cost. The stern president maintained that the component states had no right to end their association.

Faced with the disillusion of the country he cared a great deal about, Lincoln put the Constitution to the side. He invaded the South without consulting Congress, suspended *habeas corpus*, imprisoned thousands of Northern citizens without trial, shut down more than 300 newspapers, ordered the seizure of all telegrams, took un-appropriated money from the Treasury, ordered conscription, and used troops to interfere with elections. In his third year Lincoln freed the slaves in the rebellious states, but not in the border states, where he needed votes. Abolition could wait until the war was over.

Lincoln's story is tragic: a man, as much a villain as a hero, wages the ghastliest bloodletting in the history of his nation from a capital in the heart of the Confederacy, is conspired against by his Cabinet, Radical Republicans, and his generals (many of whom won't fight), and is plagued by a spendthrift and mad wife that he (possibly) infected with syphilis, thus inadvertently causing the death of two sons.

Without letting anyone suspect that he was more than a jocular, backwoods lawyer, the single-minded Lincoln gradually made himself dictator. The toll mounted steadily: Shiloh, Antietam, Gettysburg, Cold Harbor. Until the fall of Atlanta in 1864, members of his own party thought him a mediocre president and tried to replace him on the ticket with Grant.

The war slowly killed him. Much of Lincoln's famous melancholy was due to the knowledge of what he had done – 800,000 killed or wounded by the time secession was put down. Burned clean of ambition, his work done, Lincoln is ready to die and makes his fateful trip to Ford's Theatre.

The American Bismarck, Lincoln preserved the Union – and gave a "bloody and absolute rebirth to his nation." He had transformed a loosely federated republic into a highly centralized one – by destroying its soul.

Andrew Johnson attempted to continue Lincoln's moderate approach toward the South. The Radical Republicans in Congress nearly impeached Johnson and began to dictate harsh terms. President Grant used the army to suppress white insurgency in the "reconstructed" states and prop up the Republican administrations.

The adoption of the Thirteenth, Fourteenth and Fifteenth Amendments extended the vote to blacks and the Bill of Rights, officially at least, was made applicable to the states ("nor shall any State deprive any person of life, liberty, or property, without due process of law; nor deny to any person within its jurisdiction the equal protection of the laws").

The Supreme Court – on behalf of the propertied few – quickly interpreted the word "person" to apply to corporate entities and misapplied the Fourteenth Amendment to give corporations freedom from state regulation. With no federal regulation either, the corporations existed in a laissez-faire paradise. Meanwhile, the Court ignored the rights of actual human beings and civil liberties were largely left to state officialdom.

Attacked for the rampant corruption of his administration and economic depression, Grant soon lost interest in the South, as did the dwindling old abolitionist element. Southern Democrats regained power state by state, and by 1876 Federal troops remained in only South Carolina, Louisiana and Florida.

1876, the centennial year, was one of the darkest years in the history of the Republic. As the rich lived in opulence and unchecked Robber Barons amassed spectacular fortunes, poor immigrants huddled in police stations to escape the cold and maimed Civil War veterans begged in the streets. There was also the garish corruption of the Grant Administration; the war hero had planned to run for a third term but one-too-many of his army friends had bilked the US Treasury, particularly the St. Louis branch.

The presidential candidates were Samuel Tilden, a rather charmless, incorruptible reforming Democrat from New York, and a rather colorless Republican, Ohio's Rutherford B. Hayes. Tilden won the popular vote by more than 250,000 votes and appeared to carry Florida and Louisiana.

The results from Oregon, Louisiana, Florida and South Carolina were in dispute. Tilden needed one electoral vote to win. Hayes needed all twenty remaining electoral votes. Republicans controlled many of the returning boards in these states and

Grant, believing Tilden had been elected, sent troops to the three southern states to help reverse the popular vote.

For a time the country seemed to be on the brink of another Civil War. The South began to arm; the cry was "Tilden or Blood!" Yet Tilden refused to fight for his victory (or cheat the process) and spent a month preparing a history of electoral counts over the previous century. The crisis dragged on and many Southern Democrats were bought for Hayes by the railroad interests.

Early the next year a backroom bargain settled the matter. Tilden may have won the election but he would not be the 19th president. In return for the White House and continued unregulated laissez-faire capitalism, the Republicans would withdraw federal troops from the South and grant the region home rule. The election was swung to Hayes. Whites soon re-established their supremacy, the South descended into poverty, and the Negro was condemned to a century of servitude and Jim Crow. Nor was 1876 the last time that the Electoral College would subvert the popular vote.

The Gilded Age (or "Great Barbecue") had begun. The war had ended the Southern planter aristocracy and upset the political balance. Northeastern bankers and industrialists now dominated, and on their behalf, President Hayes implemented a policy of tight money. This fueled the rapid industrialization of the country but reduced much of rural America to barter. A boom and bust sequence of growth and deflation nearly destroyed the small farmer and merchant. Cheap labor, supplied by immigrants living in appalling slums, turned the US into the world's economic powerhouse by 1914. Corporations and the wealthy aggregated wealth in fewer and fewer hands and the massive gap between rich and poor made the country a plutocracy.

After the Civil War, a small, gilded group of families gradually made themselves masters of the Republic and came to own most of the country. Among the sixty leading dynasties were the houses of Rockefeller, Morgan, Harkness, Mellon, Vanderbilt, Whitney and du Pont.

This princely elite, in the words of journalist Ferdinand Lundberg, was "the living center of the modern industrial oligarchy which dominates the United States, functioning discreetly under a *de jure* democratic form of government behind which a *de facto* government, absolutist and plutocratic in its lineaments, has gradually taken form since the Civil War. This *de facto* government is actually the government of the United States – informal, invisible, shadowy. It is the government of money in a dollar democracy."

This is precisely how the United States is ruled to this day.

The behemoth that Lincoln had created had opened the way for both industrialists and world empire. The Republic was not only rich but increasingly belligerent; it wanted to expand its markets and to establish a military presence in the Far East. By 1895 the United States was filled but the Caribbean lay to the south and the Pacific to the west. All its native assets had been commodified – land, resources, and the restive labor class. The magnates wanted to enter the colonial arena occupied by their Japanese and European competitors.

Five years earlier Alfred Thayer Mahan had written the blueprint for the American Empire – *The Influence of Sea Power Upon History*. More colonies paid for more ships, and sea power was the only way for an "island nation" to prevail. Mahan argued that a failure to establish a presence in Asia would constrict US industrial capacity and lead to a "socialist" redistribution of excess production in the country. Mahan wanted to target the Caribbean, then the Pacific, and then move on to crumbling China.

Mahan's thesis greatly excited his friends Brooks Adams, a historian and grandson and great-grandson of presidents, and Theodore Roosevelt, a police commissioner in New York City. Roosevelt soon maneuvered himself into the position of assistant secretary of the navy under the mild President McKinley and went on to modernize the fleet. Hawaii and part of Samoa were annexed. Looking for enemies he set his gaze upon Spanish-ruled Cuba. "To prepare for war is the most effectual means to promote peace," TR declared in a speech.

The battleship *Maine* was blown up in Havana, Spain was held responsible, and we had "a splendid little" four-month war. In a matter of weeks, the Spanish Empire was dismantled and its Pacific and Caribbean colonies were placed under American management. The Philippines fell into US orbit, then Cuba and Puerto Rico. The US had an agreement with Filipino nationalist leader Aguinaldo to respect the Philippines' independence. Then McKinley, with God whispering in one ear, decided to annex those islands to "Christianize" them (Filipinos were

Catholic, he meant Protestantize).

Fourteen years of war against the population, and more than 200,000 dead Filipinos later, the American military had conquered the Philippines. To Roosevelt, the Filipinos were like the Apache – "savages" who must be put down in order for "prosperity" to follow. The United States was now the kind of imperial power it had once denounced.

Roosevelt's photo opportunity on Kettle Hill led to a meteoric rise – governor of New York, McKinley's running mate, and president after McKinley's assassination in 1901. America was vying with Britain, Germany, Russia, and Japan for what Roosevelt called "the domination of the world."

Mark Twain would remark that the American flag should be replaced with the Jolly Roger. "We cannot maintain an empire in the Orient and maintain a republic in America."

He was prescient.

The ruling class has a few core obsessions. The image of the masses rising up to seize the money of the few is predominant. More than three-fourths of Americans were poor or very poor. "The most difficult problem of modern times is unquestionably how to protect property under popular governments," Brooks Adams wrote. TR worried a great deal about the "have-nots," of "ignorant and unthinking people," and of the "growth of socialistic and radical spirit" among laborers. The Christian cross was increasingly appropriated as an ally of the dollar against those who would challenge and limit the rich.

The elite was never in much danger. Brooks' brother Henry knew we never had a popular government. "We have a single system," he wrote. "In that system the only question is the price at which the proletariat is to be bought and sold, the bread and circuses." A truism not for public consumption.

TR was typical of the politicians of that period and ever since. He invented the word "muckraking" to slander those journalists like Upton Sinclair who attacked the excesses of the elite. With the support of Wall Street and the party bosses, he ran against them, endeavoring to appear to be the tribune of the working-man. A loyal House of Morgan man, TR believed in concentrating wealth among the few while trying to make the few appear virtuous with some limited trust-busting. He never took on the corrupt ring that rules the Republic because he was a creature of it.

Professor Woodrow Wilson once noted that

America's system of checks and balances was the cause of most problems in the country's governance. He advocated a parliamentary system, which would be more accountable to the voters. President Wilson eagerly grasped the scepter and orb of office. He introduced Jim Crow to the capital's public places and, with the creation of the Federal Reserve, handed control of the country's money supply to Wall Street bankers.

A true believer, Wilson thought imperialism spread capitalism and morality to barbarous regions. He wanted to "teach the South American republics to elect good men," and sent troops to Nicaragua, the Dominican Republic, Mexico, Haiti, Cuba, Panama, and Honduras to bring them "freedom."

General Smedley Butler, one of the most decorated Marines in American history, later blew the whistle on the racket. Despite the rhetoric, Wilson was merely the chief enforcer for the banks:

> I spent most of my time as a high class muscle man for Big Business, for Wall Street and the bankers. In short, I was a racketeer, a gangster for capitalism. I helped make Mexico…safe for American oil interests in 1914. I helped make Haiti

and Cuba a decent place for the National City Bank boys to collect revenues in…In China in 1927 I helped see to it that Standard Oil went on its way unmolested…I might have given Al Capone a few hints. The best he could do was to operate his racket in three districts. I operated on three continents.

Fighting a war in Europe was something the old Republic had said, in the Monroe Doctrine, that it would never do. Yet Wilson's "internationalism" led him to ask Congress to declare war on Germany in April 1917 in order to "make the world safe for democracy." In actuality, the Czar's regime had fallen in Russia and America entered the war to protect J.P. Morgan's loans to the Allies. Both Congress and the placid electorate opposed the war.

Wilson promptly suspended democracy at home, instituted conscription and, to suppress dissenters, fired a broadside into the listing ship of the Constitution. The Espionage Act effectively annulled the First Amendment while the Sedition Act allowed for the deportation of foreign-born citizens (the "hyphenates" whose loyalty Wilson doubted).

George Creel, the head of the Committee of

Public Information, was charged with censoring the press and using Hollywood – that other capital of illusions – to convince the American people of the German menace. Using the crudest, most unrelenting propaganda the "Hun" was thoroughly demonized in various photo-plays.

The effort was so efficient that by July 1918, when the Germans were fifty miles west of Paris, masters of northern Italy and much of Eastern Europe, the average American believed that the US Marines were single-handedly destroying the Huns. In real life, the million American troops in France merely turned the psychological tide. At Versailles, Wilson, who seemed to want to become the first president of the world, redrew the map Europe in such a way that made inevitable another war.

Eugene Debs, the head of the Socialist Party, was imprisoned under the Espionage Act. Hollywood soon began to demonize Bolsheviks, socialists, and labor agitators as the internal enemies of "freedom." The Ku Klux Klan began to revive and establish its presence in the cities, thanks in large part to Wilson's anti-Negro and anti-immigrant policies.

The few voices that spoke for the confused majority, and were thought by business to be potentially revolutionary, were smeared as anarchists or "Reds." William Jennings Bryan, the populist leader of the Southern and Western wing of the Democratic Party was defeated all three times he stood for president. More dangerous was the idealistic La Follette of Wisconsin, with his vision of a more equitable division of power and wealth, and a new republic – one where "the people shall rule."

During the Harding, Coolidge, and Hoover Administrations the country settled back into happy isolation, and the banks and the other heavy industries ran the country as they pleased. The 1920s were a period of rampant excess, scandal, and speculative bubbles.

The expansion fueled by tight money since the 1870s began to choke on its own success. This policy had limited consumption and credit. The population in the cities had exploded, and low wages severely constrained the ability of the workers to buy the products they needed. Factories began laying off workers in an endless cycle. Shantytowns and soup kitchens were the new reality.

As Franklin Roosevelt ascended to the presidency in 1933, the structure of American society seemed to be going to pieces. A banking crisis threatened the entire monetary system, unemployment was skyrocketing, and many believed that capitalism had proven bankrupt and that "democracy" was not working. Some wanted a dictator to lift the Republic from the Great Depression. For a time the entire country was in play.

FDR embarked upon a slew of "New Deal" legislation in his first months in office, and the wealthy few feared that his abandonment of the gold standard and efforts to redistribute wealth were opening the door to Bolshevism.

In the summer of 1933 General Smedley Butler was approached by representatives of the country's wealthiest industrialists and financiers to lead an army of jobless veterans against the White House. Butler was to reduce the president to a figurehead and become the American Mussolini.

Butler played along and then exposed the plot to Congress. Several businessmen were implicated, including pro-Fascist Irénée du Pont, whose family controlled the chemical company of that name and General Motors. The big names denied everything or stayed quiet. The press, controlled by fat cats, was dismissive of both the story and the later Congressional hearings.

A committee led by John McCormack, later Speaker of the House, corroborated the essentials of

Butler's story, concluding that "certain persons had made an attempt to establish a fascist organization in this country...There is no question that these attempts were discussed, were planned, and might have been placed in execution when and if the financial backers deemed it expedient."

The story of the "Business Plot" never really broke and is largely unknown today. No one was prosecuted.

Roosevelt's goal was to restore purchasing power to the populace through transfers of wealth to consumers. The "New Deal" was underwritten by one faction of great wealth (light-goods industrialists) at the expense of another (the big banks and heavy industries). Before the 1932 election, the prescient Edmund Wilson noted in his journal:

> Hoover stands frankly for the interests of the class who live on profits as against the wage-earning classes. Franklin Roosevelt, though he speaks as a Democrat in the name of the small businessmen and farmers and is likely to be elected by them in the expectation that he can do something for them, can hardly be

imagined effecting any very drastic changes in the system which has allowed him to get into office. Whatever amiable gestures he may make, he will be largely controlled by the profit-squeezing class just as Hoover is.

The country was on the verge of something in the thirties, whether revolution or even civil war. The ascendancy of Hitler and entrenchment of Mussolini and Stalin were not lost on the Roosevelt Administration. FDR proved to be a master at playing the people, first on the radio and later in newsreels. They would crown him four times because he offered hope.

The New Deal had all the glamour of radicalism without its substance. In many cases, it harmed those most in need of help. Fundamental questions of capitalism were not in dispute, nor did FDR rein in the clans of great wealth. The Roosevelt tax measures imposed relatively high rates on the wealthy but left many loopholes for them to slip through.

There were many radical alternatives to FDR, none of which posed a greater threat than Huey Long of Louisiana – whom the president feared would split his vote for reelection in 1936. Long was a greater threat to men of property than Daniel Shays. In his "Share

Our Wealth" program Long proposed redistributing large fortunes through sharply graduated income and inheritance taxes. As he prepared to crown "every man a king," the Kingfish was gunned down by a mysterious doctor — one of those lone-nut murders than riddle American history.

A number of key features of the New Deal were struck down by Supreme Court. After his reelection, the president floated his "court-packing" proposal, which would have allowed him to name six more justices. FDR's court reform came under severe attack as an attempt to undermine the independence of the judiciary and his popularity suffered.

In the end, FDR saved capitalism from itself by accepting a degree of welfarism. Yet the New Deal did not end the Depression. Unemployment still hovered near twenty percent, and Roosevelt was only reelected in 1940 because he promised to keep America out of a foreign war — "unless attacked."

As his experiments soured FDR maneuvered the overwhelmingly isolationist country into the Second World War. Needing an excuse to go to England's aid, FDR began to push Japan, then busy conquering China and part of French Indochina, into a corner. Trade sanctions and an oil embargo were imposed by the US, costing Japan 95 percent of its oil supply.

Meanwhile, FDR ignored the attempts of Prince Konoye, the leader of the peace party, to arrange a conference.

In late November 1941, the US presented Japan with an ultimatum – to withdraw all its troops from French Indochina and China and renounce its pact with the Axis powers. The goal, according to Secretary of State Hull, was "to kick the whole thing over." The other shoe dropped when Japan, left with no alternative, attacked the fleet at Pearl Harbor.

The war ended the Depression by allowing the government to spend vast sums to build factories and hire workers. FDR was our first emperor – the American Augustus. Functioning as a dictator, the president stretched his powers to the limit and had more than 100,000 Japanese-Americans rounded up and sent to "War Relocation Camps." By war's end, FDR "had managed by force of arms and sly maneuvering to transform an isolationist republic into what no doubt would be the last empire on earth."

By 1945 America had achieved political and economic mastery of the world. Vidal summed up the choice America faced after Japan's surrender. "The United States had the choice to either disarm, as it had done in the past, and enjoy the prosperity that comes from releasing so much energy and wealth to the private sector. Or it could maintain itself on a full time military basis which would mean not only tight control over the conquered provinces of Germany, Italy and Japan but over the lives of the American people."

The war had further enriched those magnates who rule the republic, and in order to keep profits high they decided to maintain a permanent wartime footing. One of their own, Charles E. Wilson, the president of General Motors, said it best: "Instead of looking to disarmament and unpreparedness as a safeguard against war...let us try the opposite: full preparedness according to a continuing plan."

The accidental president, Harry Truman, bought this notion, which became the heart of the National Security State, as laid out in NSC-68.

But how to impose a garrison state and a militarized economy? Answer: frighten the people by invoking the Red Menace – monolithic, godless Communism forever "on the march." The Soviet threat was wildly exaggerated. We had atomic weapons; they did not. They had lost 28 million people to the war and to Stalin. Horses dragged much of their artillery back to Russia. Rather than being on the march, they were largely confined to Mitteleuropa.

They never had a chance. That the Soviet Union was no military or economic threat was immaterial. They must *seem* to be threatening.

So Truman set out to scare the American people. He stirred the pot, out of which came loyalty oaths, the House Un-American Activities Committee, McCarthyism. Conventional forces were built up, the hydrogen bomb was developed, and the military began to receive close to two-thirds of each year's federal revenue. The country was to be at perpetual war with phantom enemies within and without. In a belated fit of conscience, President Eisenhower told America that "the military-industrial complex" would change us not only politically, but spiritually. By then it was too late.

In the last 60 years, Americans have been told that some of their freedoms must be abrogated in order for the state to protect them against "enemies." Many of those rights have since been given up or systematically alienated. A new kind of country was created. The worst features of totalitarianism were imported. Now we would have a secret police (the CIA), loyalty oaths, blacklists, enemies lists, racial profiling, draconian laws, and high taxes.

Though federal endorsement of a deity or religion violated the First Amendment, the military empire embraced the military faith of Constantine. The pledge of allegiance was modified in 1954 to include the phrase "under God," and two years later "In God we trust" became the official national motto, replacing the unofficial *E pluribus unum*, and was added to paper currency beginning in 1957. Christian evangelists have increasingly forced their primitive "superstitions and hatreds upon all of us through the civil law and through general prohibitions."

Albert Einstein saw what was happening as early as 1950: "The men who possess real power in the country have no intention of ending the cold war." Korea and Vietnam followed. When the Russians did not come and the United States became the world's sole empire, new enemies were needed, and in due course, sought out. By the time of Reagan, America was reminiscent of Sparta – a militarized, increasingly xenophobic oligarchy, committed to confrontation at any cost.

This brings us to the present day.

Despite its faults, the New Deal restored a more balanced distribution of wealth and power. It was largely upheld, and expanded upon, by all the presidents from Truman to Nixon.

Since 1980 the United States has entered a Second

Gilded Age (a cynic could argue that the first one never entirely ended). In the last 30 years, the corporate rich and the banks have done everything in their power to reverse Roosevelt's bargain. Top marginal tax rates are now absurdly low. Scores of regulations – including Regulation Q and Glass-Steagall – that limited their profits have been repealed or ignored. The banking sector is once again one of the greatest power centers in the nation. They now own Capitol Hill.

The United States is as economically stratified as it was before the Depression and the oligarchs continue to counter-punch, determined to destroy what little is left of the social compact. Today the top 5 percent own 70 percent of the country's financial wealth (the top 1 percent own 42 percent). This comprises the country's ownership. The names at the top (Walton, Koch, Mars, Cargill-MacMillan) have largely changed, but the old names (du Pont, Hearst, Mellon, and Rockefeller) remain in the ranks of the super-rich. Another constant is the total contempt of the ruling class for the people.

The propertied few control the political parties which control the state which takes taxes to pay for the wars and armaments that enrich the propertied few. A small amount of revenue is returned to keep the people docile. Employing the principles of Machiavelli to maintain their power, the country's rulers keep the populace at bay with the false hope that, with a little hard work, they will one day be affluent too. The people compete for unsustainable wages, doing jobs they hate and consuming things that harm them, while their rulers maintain the country on a wartime footing and constantly search for enemies.

Policy is made by the corporate rich and their hired advisers through a web of think tanks, universities, commissions and foundations. Political parties are used to find sympathetic, ambitious people to fill offices and implement policies already formulated. Most battles over policy in government, despite all the rhetoric about the general welfare, are really disputes between different moneyed interests when the above policy planning groups cannot reach a consensus.

The people are allowed the illusion of representative government in corporately-funded quadrennial elections. It matters little whether a Republican or Democrat is elected: the ownership remains the same, and the same corporations finance both parties. Since the owners of the country own the media, these contests are kept bereft of true political debate and actual issues. Confined to received opinion, the TV talking heads chat about "process," the fetus, and the character of the candidates. Is he a *good* person? Is he cheating on his wife? Does he share "our" values?

The wasteful defense budget is inadmissible, as is the notion that the wealthy should pay far more tax than they do. Nor do they talk about the great unmentionable: that America has a ruling class. Indeed, the journalists are paid to paint an irreal picture of the country.

The owners are a very canny lot. The media is used to demonize or ridicule any threat to their monopoly of power while the state vigorously regulates our private lives, inventing prohibitions about sex, drugs and alcohol. Blood tests, urinalysis, lie detectors. None of that happened before. But who would know given our lousy education system?

"The genius of our ruling class is that it has kept a majority of the people from ever questioning the inequity of a system where most people drudge along, paying heavy taxes for which they get nothing in return" while corporations and the rich see their taxes decrease, Vidal observed.

The Supreme Court is now more of a political than a judicial entity. Its latest bit of "wisdom" – *Citizens*

United v. Federal Election Commission (2010) ruled that corporations have freedom of speech under the First Amendment, making it even easier for the biggest check writers to buy elections. Thanks to a Supreme Court that has long attacked the rights of individuals, corporations now have personhood and unlimited rights to money, and thus speech.

Meanwhile, jobs are outsourced, the health and education systems remain broken, and America's debt spirals due to imperial adventures abroad and tax cuts for the rich — paid for by taxing the non-rich and cutting their paltry services. Anything other than unfettered free-market capitalism is slandered as socialism.

Writing of England in 1783, Benjamin Franklin neatly describes America in the early 21st century

America will, with God's Blessing, become a great and happy Country; and England, if she has at length gain'd Wisdom, will have gain'd something more valuable, and more essential to her Prosperity, than all she has lost; and will still be a great and respectable Nation. Her great Disease at present is the Number and enormous Salaries and Emoluments of Office. Avarice and

Ambition are strong Passions, and separately act with great Force on the human Mind; but when both are united and may be gratified in the same Object, their Violence is almost irresistible, and they hurry Men headlong into Factions and Contentions destructive of all good Government. As long therefore as these great Emoluments subsist, your Parliament will be a stormy Sea, and your public Counsels confounded by private Interests. But it requires much Public Spirit and Virtue to abolish them! more perhaps than can now be found in a Nation so long corrupted.

It is clear that the American system, in its current form, is not worth preserving. Vidal's critics say he was a "nihilist" who tore down old conceptions without proposing alternatives. I grant that he was a master at expressing "displeasure with what is," often with a Swiftian "savage indignation." But none of it was done without proffering a reasonable alternative.

None of these critics seem to have actually read his work. If Vidal's novels described what America was, is, could have been, his essays offer a long list of proposals to fix America's malaise. In fact, he was remarkably consistent. Vidal could have taken comfort in the words of the comte de Maistre: "Toute nation a le gouvernement qu'elle mérite" (Every country gets the government it deserves). Yet he did not.

I have one of Gore's National Press Club speeches in front of me, along with his "State of the Union" essays. He starts by quoting *Common Sense* by Thomas Paine

Society in every state is a blessing, but Government, even in its best state, is but a necessary evil; in its worst state an intolerable one: for when we suffer, or are exposed to the same miseries BY A GOVERNMENT, which we might expect in a country WITHOUT GOVERNMENT, our calamity is heightened by reflecting that we furnish the means by which we suffer. Government, like dress, is the badge of lost innocence; the palaces of kings are built upon the ruins of the bowers of paradise.

One finds it hard to imagine any modern president beginning a speech with that quote. Gloomy prospect defined, Vidal made several eminently rational proposals; they amounted to nothing less than a program to recreate the Republic.

1) The four-year campaign being "a diversion for dummies," the country should limit elections to six weeks like most civilized countries. No candidate would be allowed to buy time on TV, radio, or in newspapers. The media would provide free time for the candidates to explain their policies, debate one another, etc.

2) Drastically reduce appropriations to the black hole that is the Pentagon; and, get rid of the CIA – that secret, unaccountable, and unconstitutional agency which functions as both presidential Praetorian Guard and global hit squad.

3) A movement to stop paying taxes – for the sensible reason that the people get nothing back. The education system is a wreck, the people ignorant, and the United States is the only country in the West without a health service or mass transit system.

4) "We are now locked into a class system nearly as rigid as the one that the Emperor Diocletian impressed upon the Roman Empire." The United States should do what it should have done long ago –

break up the great fortunes, redistribute the wealth of the country. Economic equality, though always viewed with contempt in Darwinist America, is the true end of a democratic society.

5) Repeal prohibitions against the sale and use of drugs. Such prohibitions feed crime, violence and most the addiction. The Volstead Act led to an enormous expansion of organized crime and alcoholism. Regulating morality doesn't work and certainly isn't the business of the state. As there will always be alcoholics there will always be drug addicts.

6) End the constitutionally questionable practice of allowing churches to be tax-exempt. Those who preach hatred against anyone who doesn't conform to their Bronze Age superstitions should have to pay their cut.

"Being a radical I want to go back to Philadelphia and do another Constitution," Vidal often said. It was the only way of fixing America's one-party dictatorship. Thomas Jefferson, the most democratic of the Founders, believed that since the Earth belongs to the living a new Constitutional Convention should be held once a generation. He did not worship his generation's handiwork.

"We might as well require a man to wear still the

coat which fitted him as a boy, as a civilized society to remain ever under the regimen of their barbarous ancestors," Jefferson wrote. Vidal pointed out that the Constitution has long been a "straightjacket" for the American people.

Article Five – the Founders' last gift to posterity – provides two methods by which the Constitution can be altered and made right. The country has only used the first way: a vote of two-thirds of both houses of Congress. The amendment is then sent for ratification by the state legislatures.

The second procedure is almost democratic. Two-thirds of the state legislatures can request a Constitutional Convention, which Congress must then convene.

If a convention was held today, the people could not be held to any single issue. The entire Constitution could be rewritten. Liberals told Vidal that the Bill of Rights will be the first thing to go; he admitted that Apple Pie fascism would lurk in the corners, but pointed out that there are many other voices in the nation. An over-zealous Supreme Court and imperial presidency have gradually eroded those rights; a new convention might act to save them.

A new convention could retain the structure of the old Republic while making significant changes. The power and prerogatives of the president should be drastically reduced, starting with the Executive Order; the archaic Electoral College should be relegated to history. The Supreme Court should be shorn of judicial review and made subservient to the laws made by the House of Representatives; the Senate transformed into an advisory group like Britain's House of Lords.

Government would rest with the House; the leader of whichever party won the most seats would become prime minister and form a cabinet composed of other representatives. New elections would be called if a sitting government lost a vote of confidence. All representatives would stand for election at the same time and all could be voted in or out. In short, America would create a parliamentary system and real political parties.

Another model for constitutional reform is the Swiss cantonal system, which could prevent any group from benefiting at the expense of another, allow for real participatory democracy and a de-centralized union – *E Unum, Pluribus.*

3

In 1982 Vidal ran for the Senate in California, using his "State of the Union" talks as a campaign speech. He spoke in favor of increased funding for education, increased taxes on corporations, and a new Constitutional Convention. He won only fifteen percent, losing to Jerry Brown in the Democratic primary and giving up any hope of election to high office. Becoming a senator, or even president, was the great "unfinished business" of his life. Yet he never really wanted to spend his late fifties and early sixties in the Senate or give up his writing. Winning was not as important as airing ideas.

Instead, Vidal continued to transform his public persona into that of a ruler in exile. Away from the nation he considered woefully under-civilized, Gore carved out his own bit of civilization. Italy remained a congenial place to study his native country. Though he was disenchanted by Italy's alliance with the American Empire, he could understand how it benefited from America's global ambitions.

"After the war a good deal of American money was given to rebuild Italy, and that was a good thing even if the Mafia and/or the politicians got too large a commission," Gore wrote his friend Judith Harris. "Since then, I can't think of any American institution that contributes much of anything to Italy. I suppose that the fleet at Gaeta, and the air force at Vicenza, serve as a deterrent to Soviet ambition...And I suspect that even those Italians who do not love America sometimes have nightmares of Tito dead and Soviet troops staring hungrily at Trieste and points south."

The Ravellesi didn't know what to make of Gore and Howard at first, driving into town in their Jaguar, wearing cowboy hats, and accompanied by a yappy terrier. "They kind of loved it you see," Howard said. Of their first half-decade in Ravello, Gore recalled that the villagers would "still speak of us as the 'two English sculptors.'" They would come to know three generations of Ravellesi.

La Rondinaia soon became an intellectual and social salon, a place of pilgrimage for literati and celebrities. If Vidal could not become president, he could still hold court as emperor in exile. From the villa's balcony, he was lord of all he surveyed – the swallows, the lemon trees and the wide expanse of opal blue sea.

Howard looked after the household and the finances, giving Gore time to work. Gore was not naturally social (he was easily bored by small talk) and Howard helped there too. Most evenings Gore and Howard entertained guests at one of the local trattorias like Zaccaria (his favorite) or Vittoria. Friends wondered whether gastronomy was Gore's true passion. Back at La Rondinaia, bottles of local wine would give way to scotch. While many of the guests began to slur, Gore seemed to grow more lucid and articulate with drink.

Unlike the aloof Graham Greene on Capri, Vidal embraced Italian life. Christopher Hitchens once called him "the Pope of Ravello." Gore and Howard regularly sat at the café, entertaining the locals with stories. The Ravellesi, and the inhabitants of the neighboring villages, called him "il Maestro" or "lo Scrittore" – the writer.

They greeted him obsequiously, often bowing as he passed by; such gestures were returned by a polite Vidal, who would bow his head and praise Italy for its warmth and hospitality (Vidal learned to read Italian, but never spoke it well). He served on the local booster council and supported left-wing political figures in the village. His generosity was legendary and he often paid medical bills or school expenses for the locals. The Ravellesi still speak of it all these years later.

Having become something of a prisoner of his youthful, handsome persona, Vidal began to eat and drink as he liked. Life was not attractive enough to compete with such sensual pleasures. "In restaurants he quit ordering salads and sneaking French fries off other people's plates," his friend Michael Mewshaw recalled. "He asked for what he wanted and ate it all, and when he grew fat, he accepted that this was how it was meant to be. No more dieting and going to the gym."

Vidal once said: "Some writers take to drink, others take to audiences." In the eighties he embraced both with a new vigor. In addition to great amounts of wine, Mewshaw recalled Gore drinking "Falstaffian portions of Scotch and vodka." He was diabetic and his blood pressure soon suffered. For years he had been vilified as a narcissist; now he was called slovenly. Vidal didn't care, or claimed not to, and became "permanently heavy."

His old wicked sense of humor had not withered.

107

In fact, his barbs sharpened. In Ronald Reagan the American corporations had finally found an actor who could read his lines. "Prepare yourself for some bad news" Gore announced on the Carson show. "Ronald Reagan's library just burned down. Both books were destroyed. But the real horror: he hadn't finished coloring either one of them." As for the death of Truman Capote, Vidal said: "Well that was a good career move."

To those who invaded his privacy he would be stunningly confessional, and those who bored him would find that he had his own transgressive way of enlivening conversations. During one dinner party at Mewshaw's Roman apartment, Andrea Lee talked to Gore about her new novel *Sarah Phillips* (1984) and how much their mutual editor Jason Epstein loved her work.

Jason was one of Gore's oldest friends but their friendship was crumbling under creative differences. Epstein disliked Gore's inventions like *Myra* and *Kalki*, preferring the best-selling historical reflections.

Lee prattled on and Gore cut in, "Has anyone noticed that as a man gets older, his wee-wee begins to grow back into his body."

She was baffled – and earnest.

"Don't you think your body is, you know, gaining

weight and growing down around your penis so it just looks like its growing back into you?"

"No, it's retreating," Gore said.

At parties in the early eighties Vidal frequently declared that he was tired and wanted to die. This left Howard agitated and he often left the room. Vidal was convinced that young writers couldn't wait for the older generation to die off. An off-and-on depression plagued him for the rest of his life. Despite his money, fame and millions of readers there was so much left undone. His political aspirations were dead, and his Roman stoicism could only do so much to mask the many small slights and rejections. So he medicated himself with more and more drink.

As Vidal was bringing *Lincoln* to a close in the early autumn of 1983 his friends began to descend on Ravello for a special occasion. Not long after Gore's 58th birthday, Ravello made him an honorary citizen. He was "proud as a peacock" according to one friend. Local and national dignitaries came, as did prominent Italian writers like Luigi Barzini, Alberto Arbasino, and Italo Calvino – the last of whom Vidal admired more than any of his contemporaries.

The ceremony, performed by Ravello's mayor, with the customary grand speeches and panegyrics to edenic Ravello, was held in the gardens of the Villa Rufolo. All the guests received a basket of lemons from Vidal's terraces. Calvino said Vidal had "never left America even for one second. His passionate and polemical participation in American life is without interruption."

"There was singing (Cantore di Napoli) in the square, colored lights, the works. I suppose now they will try to get as much mileage out of me as they do from Wagner," Gore wrote one friend. Ravello remained proud of its association with Vidal, which brought tourist dollars to the village and international publicity.

All the guests returned to La Rondinaia for a house party. For Mewshaw it was the occasion that Gore emerged from his depression.

Vidal had begun to sum up his life-story by quoting Flaubert (who was quoting Horace) – "He remained at home and wrote." That was indeed the pattern of his life at La Rondinaia during the eighties and nineties. Less and less time was being spent in Rome.

Creativity was the one thing to believe in, in a world that Vidal believed should be liberated from monotheistic faith. Despite his complaints about decreasing energy, his output did not slacken between

1985 and 2000. Like Flaubert he prepared texts and denied the significance of his own personality, questing relentlessly for "le mot juste" and the perfect turn of phrase.

Yet his work would not be treated with the seriousness that it deserved. Academic "scholar squirrels" attacked Vidal on minutiae and were savaged by him in response. They could not fathom that he was writing, not for graduate students or literati, but for the masses. This seemed an ideal way to get his message out; as a writer he had far more political influence and freedom to speak out than he would have had as a senator.

The message was failing to get through. Vidal knew that the right-wing crowd would always hold him in contempt, and he reciprocated. Yet his blunt appraisal of America, mistrust of its elites, and his knowledge that they don't mean well and commit evil acts, was difficult for many ordinary Americans to handle. Vidal blamed a dreadful education system that feeds patriotic platitudes to the ignorant young and a media, owned by a handful of corporations, which inflicts "a drip-torture of misinformation" upon them as they become parents themselves.

"I didn't mean to spend my life writing American history, which should have been taught in the schools, but I saw no alternative but to taking it on myself. I could think of a lot of cheerier things I'd rather be doing than analyzing George Washington and Aaron Burr. But it came to pass, that was my job, so I did it."

Vidal continued to forge ahead, scolding America for what it is and could have been, but with a growing weariness. It was an attitude of How-did-it-become-my-problem-to-point-out-society's-failures?

I remember one of *Time* Magazine's least bilious features on Vidal was titled "Laughing Cassandra." Though he found less and less to laugh about, the Cassandra part was ideal, for like the beautiful figure of Greek mythology he was blessed with the gift of prophecy. Gore's curse, like Cassandra's, was that he could see what was coming but was forced to watch powerlessly as his warnings were ignored.

For Vidal there was always a ready answer:

To be demoralized by the withdrawal of public success (a process as painful in America as the withdrawal of a drug from an addict) is to grant too easy a victory to the society one has attempted to criticize, affect, change, reform. It is clearly unreasonable to expect to be cherished by those one assaults. It is also childish, in the deepest sense of being a child, ever to expect justice. There is none beneath our moon. One can only hope not to be entirely destroyed by injustice and, to put it cynically, one can very often flourish through an injustice obtaining in one's favor. What matters finally is not the world's judgment of oneself but one's own judgment of the world. Any writer who lacks this final arrogance will not survive long in America.

Torn between the Hegelian view of Henry Adams (entropy, history is made up of great currents, in the long view the race will be gone) and the liberalism of his old friend and neighbor Eleanor Roosevelt (in the short term things can be done), Vidal chose the latter.

Unlike the old WASPs Vidal liked the flow of immigrants. He believed that the new mix of people combined with the Bill of Rights could lead to a "phoenix-like return," but that our metamorphosis was at least a century away (that was said in 1990). He had to believe America was still in the process of being made.

"I'm a populist, from a long line of tribunes to the

people. And I believe the government, to be of any value, must rest upon the people at large, and not be the preserve of any elite group or class, or anything of a hereditary nature," he said.

That year, with the publication of *Hollywood*, Vidal admitted what many might have suspected: that he was writing one long book, an American epic, its Odyssey. No one had tried it before. He never announced such a grand design, for loss of energy or death could have intervened. The nineties seem like halcyon days, at least in retrospect, though he may not have agreed. He was, after all, in the "springtime of my senility," and there were several health crises and his own hypochondria. But he was still at work.

In 1990 Vidal wrote *Theodora*, for Universal and Martin Scorsese. "Theodora, a prostitute, marries the Emperor Justinian, and between them, they restore the Roman Empire," he said. He toyed around with writing a novel on the subject. Gore talked about the project throughout the early nineties and Scorsese liked the script, but the film was never made.

He was also tempted to extend his American series to the era of Lyndon Johnson – "a more interesting figure" than Kennedy. He had a character in mind who would have seen the empire fall on its face in Korea and Vietnam. Not wanting to write "such a sad book" he turned instead to a new "invention" – his culminating lampoon of Judeo-Christianity.

Live from Golgotha (1992) was a "happy book, with a happy ending." NBC goes back in time to shoot the "actual crucifixion, resurrection, the whole ball of wax...Live." There is a corporate takeover of most media by the Japanese. Meanwhile, a computer hacker tries to eliminate all records of Christianity's existence. There will be no more Jesus, only the Japanese Mother Goddess.

Monotheism, that "great unmentionable evil at the center of our culture," insulted his intelligence and warred against all who believe differently; moreover, its followers were carriers of Oriental despotism. The three faiths that grew out of the Old Testament – that "barbaric Bronze Age text" – were fundamentally anti-human. The end of monotheism was the beginning of civilization.

"Christianity was acknowledged "officially" as a Jewish heresy by Archbishop Temple some 50 years ago. Judaism in turn seems to be a Zoroastrian heresy (with Egyptian additions) as demonstrated in *Creation*. I dislike all forms of monotheism because the notion of one arbitrary god-creator inevitably becomes totalitarian in earthly politics – one ruler, one Pope, one factory boss, one father as head of family, etc.

…This leads to all sorts of evil, as Freud grasped."

The following year Vidal's *United States: Collected Essays 1952-1992* was published. He felt that the reception was lukewarm, but the thick tome did win a National Book Award. In 1993 Gore and Howard abandoned the Rome apartment. The city was boring them, the rent was high, the pollution unbearable. New windows were put in La Rondinaia to make it habitable all year round, and there was also the house in the Hollywood Hills.

He had begun to work on his memoirs – "Me-Mores" as he called them. Though he swore he would never look back he found himself doing just that. Instead of writing about himself, he wrote absorbingly of others – as he had always done.

He would call the book *Palimpsest* – "a parchment, etc., which has been written upon twice; the original writing having been rubbed out" but still partially readable. It was a metaphor for the "archaeological layers of a life to be excavated like the different levels of old Troy, where, at some point beneath those cities upon cities, one hopes to find Achilles and his beloved Patroclus."

There was a great revelation. Gore's other "great unfinished business" was that he had never recovered from the death of Jimmie Trimble at Iwo Jima.

"For years," he writes, 50 years on, "I would address the night: 'Jimmie, are you anywhere?' and almost always the wind would rise. I am neither a believer in the afterlife nor a mystic. Yet I still want Jimmie to be, somewhere, if only on this page."

Palimpsest was published was on his 70th birthday in 1995, and was a revelation for the Trimble material alone. "Finally, I seem to have written, for the first and last time, not the ghost story that I feared, but a love story, as circular in shape as desire (and its pursuit), ending with us whole at last in the shade of a copper beech."

He had bought a plot in Washington's Rock Creek Cemetery, where Trimble was buried.

The old rake's greatest pleasure, aside from writing, came from good food and drink. "One gets more done without drinking," he told his friend Judith Halfpenny in the summer of 1990, "and the memory blossoms but I shall resume once I've remembered all I want to, and sink myself into whiskey where one's sense of time is so altered that one feels in the moment immortality – a long luminous present which, not drinking, becomes a fast-moving express train named…Nothing."

Sometimes Vidal went off alcohol to lose weight for public appearances or book tours, or if a medical problem made it necessary. He resumed as quickly as possible. "I drank like a boy all summer, until I looked again like Farouk," he wrote Halfpenny the following year.

He found that there were "no compensations" in getting older. "The work will soon be done, I suppose there's a sense of relief there, except one likes to do the work. One fascinating thing about age is that, at least in my case, you have no fear of death at all."

During the second half of the nineties, Gore wrote *The Golden Age*, the last of his American novels. It was an attempt to get right what he believed he had failed to convey in *Washington, D.C.* – the sense of a republic turning into an empire. The book focused on the pivotal events of his generation: Pearl Harbor, the war, the bomb, and Truman's creation of the National Security State. The novel was published in 2000, the year that saw the revival of *The Best Man* on Broadway. What should have been an *annus mirabilis* instead proved to be an absolute horror.

Ravello was still "the perfect place to read and write," and to pronounce his oracles from atop his personal Parnassus. The village priest came to bless La Rondinaia, room by room, according to local tradition. There was coffee and the reading of mail with Howard at the Bar San Domingo, where they kept up with every plot and subplot of town gossip. The village had endeavored to beautify itself in the late nineties; now the piazza had new paving stones and the cathedral had been "ruthlessly restored." Two local battles were lost: Vidal had argued passionately for the building of a cable railway and against the Oscar Niemeyer-designed auditorium – a spaceship-like structure that now mars the medieval village.

Vidal spoke of history as if he had been there, as if he had seen it all before. Declining empires had debt, an overstretched military, too much religion, and corrupted language ("Words are used to disguise, not to illuminate, action: you liberate a city by destroying it. Words are to confuse, so that at election time people will solemnly vote against their own interests").

Vidal had lived through "about one-third of the history of the United States of America," which he had "always regarded as a family affair." He remembered his grandfather telling him about conversations he had with Lincoln's son Robert – how Robert recalled his father as being a very cold man. And he knew and loved his country's history as well, often better, than did academics.

The presidential election of 2000 was an eerie

reprise of 1876. At the millennium, Vidal's bicentennial novel was sadly relevant. Albert Gore, a distant relative, won the popular vote by 0.5 percent. Again the Florida electoral votes would be crucial, and the voice of the people would be silenced. Votes were invalidated more often in black districts, like Miami-Dade, than white.

The election was purloined for Bush by a 5-4 majority in the Supreme Court (Justice Scalia's son represented Bush before the Court), which brazenly created a series of calculated delays to prevent the counting of ballots. There was no more time the justices said in December. The *Miami Herald* concluded that Al Gore had won Florida by 23,000 votes. But the loser of the election would be inaugurated. Justice John Paul Stevens said that the true loser was "the nation's confidence in the judge as an impartial guardian of the rule of law."

Vidal was left to contemplate "a powerless Mikado ruled by a shogun vice president and his Pentagon warrior counselors." Bush did what the owners of the country hired him to do – cut their taxes (individual rates, capital gains, dividends, estate) – and then retired to Crawford, Texas for the summer of 2001 and cleared brush.

Then came the shock of 9-11. Vidal called it "a

pretext for getting rid of the Republic, replacing it with a dictatorial system as best personified by the USA Patriot Act which removes us of our Bill Rights." The act eroded the First, Fourth, Fifth, Sixth, Eighth and Fourteenth Amendments. Enhanced interrogation (i.e. torture), rendition, and airport security joined the Orwellian panoply. Then came the wars for oil...but the sad story is well known. Freedom sacrificed for the illusion of security. The young, even the middle-aged, accept it – they are too young to remember what it was like to live in a free country.

"We have ceased to be a nation under law but instead a homeland where the withered Bill of Rights, like a dead trumpet vine, clings to our pseudo-Roman columns," Vidal wrote – a lonely voice, as he had always been, crying out in the wilderness. "Happily for the busy lunatics who rule over us, we are permanently the United States of Amnesia. We learn nothing because we remember nothing."

Though hobbled by a bad knee Vidal traveled around the country, continuing to speak and defy. Nonetheless, he had largely lost faith in a populace that is being screwed by the wealthy and too addled by McDonald's and reality TV to do anything about it. Today America is not only a corporate state but a zero-sum society – where what benefits the ruling elite harms the rest of us.

The reign of Bush, America's twelfth and most oafish Caesar, confirmed all of Vidal's fears. The strains of overseas conquest had ended America's Republic, as they had ended Rome's. Empire would inevitably result in the decline of democracy. It was only a matter of time before the strain of governing the world caused the empire to collapse as well. In the long run, I expect that historians of the future (if there are any) will look to Vidal, and a small handful of others, to make sense of our refuse.

"One day I think [the people] are going to rise up and tear this damn thing to pieces. Would that I were young and it was spring…To be there."

In Russian, "gore vidal" means "he has seen grief;" there was certainly plenty of that in his last dozen years. As the national tragedy unfolded, Gore watched as Howard, his companion of 53 years, slowly died of lung cancer. "Didn't it go by awfully fast?" Howard asked him near the end. In 2003 "'we' ceased to be we and became 'I.'"

Late autumn had given way to winter.

Gore finished a second memoir, *Point to Point Navigation* (2006), in which, as one reviewer pointed out, he drank up the rest of his wine cellar on the page. Memory and death was the motif; he grieved the death of friends until he was the only one left. The figures that reoccur throughout – Tennessee Williams, Johnny Carson, Saul Bellow, Paul Bowles, and Federico Fellini – were all gone. Vidal told his last stories as if he was trying to mathematically cancel himself out until there was nothing left to say. He was surrounded by ghosts: his bitch mother, Jack Kennedy, Jimmie Trimble, Howard.

That same year Vidal sold La Rondinaia and returned to the Hollywood Hills for what he called his "Cedars-Sinai years." Pedestrian Ravello, with its many steps and paths, was no longer attractive to an octogenarian with a titanium knee. Nor could the village, or the hospital in Salerno, provide the medical attention he required. He regretted leaving Italy and returned often. In his late senescence, he bought a house in Le Tignet, a dusty village near Grasse in the south of France, and spent a little time there.

"As I now move graciously, I hope, toward the door marked Exit," he begins one sentence in that last memoir. But he didn't. He had lived too long. He had begun to quote a line William Dean Howells wrote to Henry James: "I am comparatively a dead cult with my statues cut down and the grass growing over me in pale moonlight."

The filter went; he said stupid things. The hawk in search of prey was now cornered by Time, the final predator; he was now "all beak like a new-hatched eagle" as he had once described the dying Christopher Isherwood. The old wit was replaced with sour misanthropy and cold rage. How did he want to be remembered? One day it was as a writer of perfect sentences; another, "I don't give a goddamn."

By 2009 Gore was re-reading Thucydides, to remind himself how Athens had lost its empire and its liberty, and continuing to talk about a novel about the Mexican War – the one period he felt he had missed out on.

Late that year, at the National Book Awards dinner in Manhattan, Gore received the medal for Distinguished Contribution to American Letters. There would be no Pulitzers, no Nobels. Such is the fate of contrarians. Those honors are reserved for the tenured "hacks of academe" by a self-serving establishment. He was feeble and wheelchair-bound that night, his voice hushed.

Joanne Woodward was there to introduce him. Many years earlier Gore stood as godfather to her and Paul's first baby. Joanne told the story: the baby was sprinkled as Gore held her gingerly; after a moment's pause, he looked down and said: "Always a godfather, never a God."

The crowd laughed.

"But now you are!" Joanne said. Gore threw his arms up, the audience roared. And he smiled that old wry grin.

Body had faded and then, tragically, mind. Alzheimer's did its malignant work. There would be no more novels, no more essays. A year or so later he stopped writing. There was no one left to impress, he said. He loved conversation and there was much less of that now. He stayed up late, nursing a Glenfiddich and listening to tapes of Howard singing show tunes. Then dementia, his nephew Burr Steers wrote, "robbed my uncle of his soul-saving sense of irony, without which he was unrecognizable."

Vidal spent the last four months of his life in bed. The last book he read was *The Wizard of Oz.* Pneumonia set in and he entered the long night on a Tuesday – July 31, 2012. He was buried next to Howard in Rock Creek Cemetery, in the capital where he spent his youth. Their plots are midway between Jimmie Trimble and Henry Adams – "midway between heart and mind."

Looking back on his work Vidal found that "there

is a great deal about ending, a great deal about death. I think, in a way, death is the most interesting of subjects...But ultimately it is how you live in time, time is what literature is about. And time must have a stop."

In his attempts to understand death he found solace, not in the promise of an afterlife, but in the atomists, Lucretius and Democritus – "that death is a dissolution and the idea of this personality continuing is not only ridiculous but tragic." But also that "we are forever part of the universe, like it or not, the atoms that comprise each one of us, that comprise every galaxy all came from the same source" and that the matter that makes us up continues, goes into new arrangements.

"Because there is no cosmic point to the life that each of us perceives on this distant bit of dust at the galaxy's edge ..." he once said, "... there is all the more reason for us to maintain in proper balance what we have here. Because there is nothing else. No thing. This is it. And quite enough, all in all."

His final consolation came from his stained, well-thumbed copy of Montaigne:

If we have not known how to live, it is not
right to teach us how to die, making the

form of the end incongruous with the whole. If we have known how to live steadfastly and calmly we shall know how to die the same way...death is indeed the ending of life, but not therefore its end: it puts an end to it, it is its ultimate point: but it is not its objective. Life must be its own objective, its own purpose...Numbered among its other duties included under the general and principal heading, How to Live, there is the subsection, How to Die.

Writing was done to impose some order on the flux of sensations and experiences we call life – "to hold something, the past the present," and ultimately, an "action against death." That Vidal had a very highly developed sense of an ending not only heightened his pleasure in life but allowed him to write stunning literary codas.

At the end of *Julian*, the emperor's old teacher Libanius sits at home in Antioch and realizes that the old pagan world has ended. Christian fanaticism will soon triumph. "The barbarians are at the gate," Libanius wrote. "Yet when they breach the wall, they will find nothing of value to seize. The spirit of what we were has fled."

I have been reading Plotinus all evening. He has the power to soothe me; and I find his sadness curiously comforting. Even when he writes: "Life here with the things of earth is a sinking, a defeat, a failing of the wing." The wing has indeed failed. One sinks. Defeat is certain. Even as I write these lines, the lamp wick sputters to an end, and the pool of light in which I sit contracts. Soon the room will be dark. One has always feared that death would be like this. But what else is there? With Julian, the light went, and now nothing remains but to let the darkness come, and hope for a new sun and another day, born of time's mystery and man's love of light.

Surveying his domain for the last time, our Prospero was, ever and always, an optimist:

As for the human case, the generation of men come and go and are in eternity no more than bacteria upon a luminous slide, and the fall of a republic or the rise of an empire—so significant to those involved—

128

are not detectable upon the slide even were there an interested eye to behold that steadily proliferating species which would either end in time or, with luck, become something else, since change is the nature of life, and its hope.

For over half a century Gore Vidal crafted perfect sentences — shattering pieties, exposing the powerful, and exalting the human over the inhuman. Though he has entered a new cycle of creation, the words are there, for all to find, and deserve to be read as long as the disappearing republic he loved and loathed endures — beacons of light, like the mind of their creator, to illuminate a darkened sea.